Craig .

Cracking the Apostolic & Prophetic

CODE

Daniel 7:18, 22, 27

The Master Combination for Kingdom and Global Dominance of ALL World Systems!

APOSTOLIC

PROPHETIC

Matt 21:43

PALM TREE PUBLICATIONS
A Division of Palm Tree Productions

PUBLISHED BY PALM TREE PUBLICATIONS
A DIVISION OF PALM TREE PRODUCTIONS
KELLER, TEXAS U.S.A.
PRINTED IN THE U.S.A.
www.palmtreeproductions.net

Palm Tree Productions is a Media Services Company dedicated to seeing the Kingdom of God advanced by ministries and businesses with excellence, integrity, and professionalism through the use of high quality media resources. Whether the publication is print, audio, or visual, we are dedicated to excellence in every aspect from concept to final production.

Cover Design: Wendy K. Walters

Cover Photos: Courtesy of Big Stock Photos

Cracking the Apostolic & Prophetic C O D E

ISBN: 978-0-9817054-3-X
LIBRARY OF CONGRESS CONTROL NUMBER: 2008936706

To contact the author:

Wealth Builders Advisory Group, Inc.
2111 El Camino Real, Suite 202
Oceanside, CA 92054

1-800-908-7065
Info@WealthBuildersAdvisoryGroup.com

ℬ ℭ

DEDICATION

ℬ ℭ

I'd like to dedicate this book to my beautiful wife and best friend, Darlene, whom I have had the privilege of being with since I was 19 years old. I will never forget the first time that I laid eyes on you, and you are even more beautiful and attractive to me today than you were almost 26 years ago. It is because of your prayers, faith, and decrees that I am alive today and not in hell. You often tell me that now your calling in life is to keep me out of trouble. Thank God for an apostolic and prophetic wife. You are not only God's prophet, but you are my prophet. Know how much I love and adore you. I would never have made it this far without you. You are my everything!

I also want to dedicate this book to my three sons; Robert, Craig Jr., and Matthew. They have had the great fortune (and misfortune) of living with me and tolerating me all of their lives as I was growing and developing as a father, a person, a prophet, a businessman, and now as an apostle. I can honestly and truly say that I have the most handsome and best sons in the world. It is because of them that I do my best to live holy and righteous before God, so that they can be the best men of God and that they will excel in their generation! Growing up, my sons did not give me a third of the problem that I gave to my parents—and that is why they are blessed and shall live long on the earth.

I'd like to thank both of my parents, James and Imogene Ponder, who both died at very young ages. My dad passed away at the age of 48, and my mother at age 56. They provided the best lifestyle and childhood that a son could ever ask for. It was my father's style, work habits, and family vacation trips that shaped me into a husband and father. It was my mother's class, charm, stubbornness, love, and sophistication that made me the man that I am today. I miss you both greatly, but I have a great family, and it is all because of the great values that you put inside of me from an early age. Thank you.

Lastly, I dedicate this book to parents. I charge you to never give up on your children. Our children are our only hope of having a successful future generation! Bless them with your mouth, bless them with your finances, and bless them with your love!

ℰℴ ℭℛ

ACKNOWLEDGEMENTS

ℰℴ ℭℛ

I first want to acknowledge the power of God, and His transforming Word in my life. After spending over a year working on this book, something very unusual happened to me. On June 27, 2008, I had the privilege of speaking at Apostle John Eckhardt's Annual IMPACT Conference. This year's theme was "Apostolic Strategies from Generation To Generation." During the conference, God began to deal with me very strongly regarding the next generation. He told me that this book was not written just for those that are in the marketplace, or for my generation, but also to the next generation. He instructed me to, "put the revelation and the release of the Kingdom into their hands."

Had I had known this before I began, I don't believe that I would have written the book in the way that I did. The language is strong, almost forceful in places. Is it too tough for our youth? When the youth of this generation are forced to join a gang, they are "jumped in" (must take a physical beating) as early as age 8. Young girls and boys are pressured to have sex—even oral sex in elementary school, and encouraged to try drugs at a very early age. On top of this, they are offered help from a seemingly powerless church—one that has not really operated in signs and wonders, and has produced very few sons and daughters. Many have parents who rarely tell them that they love them, or how proud they are of them. Sadly, many youth have parents who don't really listen to them, or rarely sit down and take the time to have a real conversation with them. When I consider this perspective, then maybe I didn't write this book strongly enough! But, as long as there is breath in my body, I REFUSE for any person of the next generation not to know what their rights, privileges, and benefits are in the Kingdom. Even more, I want them to understand how to OPERATE in the Kingdom! Some think that offering kids the nursery, children's church, or a youth class will change the world—but that is NOT the pattern God told me and my wife to reproduce. God told us to take the revelation of this book and the release of the Kingdom, and to place it into their hands.

It is my desire, my prayer, and my passion that you will covenant with me, have kingly vision and insight to be able to see what young person you should share this book with. It doesn't matter if they are quiet and introverted, rebellious and confused, or bright and on the ball. Remember YOU are placing the KINGDOM in their hands so that they can REPENT, CHANGE, and take over the world!

I would like to personally thank Prophetess Francine King from Equipping the Saints International in Yucaipa, CA. In November 2006, she was the first one that opened up a door for us in the marketplace. You never know who God is going to use, and I will never forget the favor, grace, and respect that you have showed to me and my family. I am glad to still be in covenant with you and like I said when I first met you, "You are like the sister that I never had," and always remember—we have your back!

I would also like to thank all of the haters, critics, doubters, and enemies—especially all of those from the four-walled church who didn't believe in me. It was because of your rejection that I began to seek God deeper and for more. It was my prayer to Him that if He would bless me, deliver me, and bring me out and establish me in the Kingdom, I would never forget where I came from. I promised God to help others not to make the same mistakes that I did.

I would also like to thank all of those that attended and were a part of our Prophetic Gathering in Oceanside, CA. It was you, your lives, and your belief in me that helped increase my level of maturity and revelation—to quickly accelerate them so that the Kingdom of God would be established in this generation and in the generations to come.

I would like to personally thank Apostle John Eckhardt, my spiritual father and primary covering. I thank Crusaders Church and the IMPACT Network, their staff, and volunteers that have been so good to my family and me. You have always treated us just like family from day one—especially Prophet Shirene Anderson, who from the very beginning has been an encouragement and a true apostolic prophet that cares, covers, and establishes.

To Apostle John P. Kelly, I want to personally thank you for also being an apostolic connection and for believing in me and my family. You stepped into my life when I needed new order, a new platform, and a grace to go higher in the Kingdom economically. What a ride we are in for!

Lastly, I would like to personally thank all of those who took the time to write an endorsement. All these people took time out of their very busy schedules to read the book, consider its message, and then give me their endorsement.

Some were unwilling to give an endorsement, and I must admit that I was shocked and saddened by some of their responses—but then I remembered that I am confronting the three gates of hell! A few individuals were under deadlines and had other obligations. These asked if they could submit their endorsement later for when I would run a second printing of the book, and I appreciate their input as well.

So, to all those who did read the manuscript and write an endorsement, my wife and I are forever thankful and grateful to you and your ministry. We release Kingdom blessings to you. We release fresh strength and grace over your marriages, and new open doors of opportunity and wealth over your personal finances and the finances of your ministries. We pray that God will give you greater revelation and greater insight into the Kingdom, and that God would establish you greater in the apostolic and the prophetic. We pray that He will expand your borders, and believe that there will be a release of new spiritual sons and daughters into your ministry!

TABLE OF CONTENTS

ॐ ॐ

___

FOREWORD BY
APOSTLE JOHN ECKHARDT

___

ॐ ॐ

Prophet Craig Ponder is one of those rare ministers who understand the Kingdom of God and the importance of Apostolic and Prophetic Ministries.

This book will help any believer understand the importance of revelation as a key to prosperity and abundant life. His personal journey to breakthrough will encourage you to persevere until your breakthrough comes. This is not the time to be an ordinary believer, but the time to be extraordinary and crack the Apostolic and Prophetic Code. I was thoroughly impressed with his revelation on the Kingdom and also how he broke down the apostolic and the prophetic. The truths in this book helped me to think "outside the box," and I believe they will challenge you to go further into new realms of prosperity.

It is time to break out of the four walls of the church. Now is the time to become Kingdom minded. Don't be limited by tradition, but break free and walk in truth and revelation. I highly endorse this book, and encourage all believers to read it and draw from the insights of Craig Ponder in order to enjoy Kingdom advancement and breakthrough.

Apostle John Eckhardt

Apostle and Overseer of Crusaders Church, Chicago, IL

Founder and Presiding Apostle of IMPACT Network

Author of more than 30 books including
"Moving In the Apostolic"

Author's Note

Apostle John Eckhardt is a pioneer and reformer who is considered by many to be the father of the apostolic.

ဆဉ ဌ

FOREWORD BY
APOSTLE JOHN P. KELLY

ဆဉ ထ

The church is standing at a precipice of a new change—a change of wineskin. Those being led desire to be used in more significant ways, have more of a voice, and a greater input. Those leading desire that those they have charge over would have more knowledge and exercise more discipline. The reality is that both groups have a valid perspective.

God is shaking the Church as well. Scripture tells us that all things that can be shaken will be shaken. The church is split into a minimum of a thousand different sects called denominations. Beyond this, non-denominational groups split up into even more sects. Without question, there is evidence that the religionists and traditionalists have taken control over much of the Church. Some churches have become nothing more than social centers. Others have become places for political expression. Still others are so mystical that they have completely lost touch with reality.

I see these issues as challenges that need to be confronted and clarified. What many see as disruptions, I see as opportunities for a new and greater Church. I see them as a catalyst to bring about a better and brighter future for the Church. In order to overcome these things, the dividing walls within the church must be torn down, and the knowledge that we are all called to the work of the ministry must be promoted by all.

We are not all called to minister in or to a local church. Only a very few are meant for this. The majority are called to minister in the marketplace and in the workplace. The five-fold gifts are to reproduce themselves into the lives of the believers that they may become saints who are warring to expand the Kingdom of God in the workplace and in the marketplace. In order to do this, the saints must be raised up. This means that they are trained and educated in how to war a warfare in all realms of society—religion, education, government, media, arts and entertainment, business, and the family. We must do this by using wisdom, knowledge, and understanding to enter the high places of the workplace and the marketplace, tear them down, and establish the dominion of God.

Churches have done a good job in raising up servants. Sadly, some have raised up slaves. All of us are called to be servants, to understand how to serve the King, and how to be a steward of all that we have dominion over. We truly are possessors of nothing. Everything we have at any given moment could be required of us by Him to give—whether this be our clothes, our cars, our time, our finances... But the Church must go beyond raising up servants. The Church must raise up kings and priests. The Church must raise up men and women of godly character who are trained and educated both in spiritual things and in secular things. The Church must release the saints. She must recognize that they are anointed and appointed into their assignments within the workplace and marketplace. Hands must be laid on them and they must be commissioned by God and by the ministers of the Church into this mission field called the world.

Yes, it is a spiritual warfare, but it is also a secular and practical warfare as well. Its strategies are spiritual and strategic, but they are also physical and executable. Too many times, churches get involved in making decisions, but never call in people with expertise who are right there within their own church body. I have encountered many church leaders who feel a great need to resemble the "All-in-All." They feel like they are expected to be knowledgeable on all topics. How else can they be called the leader unless they are out in front of the pack? These leaders are fooling no one but the uneducated and inexperienced. Those with knowledge and expertise are fully aware that they are all "bluff and blunder" and little substance.

This doesn't mean they don't know something, but often leaders speak in headlines and skip the vital content. It would be better to say, "I don't know about this. Can you give me some information, or direct me to a book or resource where I can learn more?" In fact, instead of this weakening the leader, it would strengthen the relationship between him and those he is leading. It demonstrates that you lead where you are qualified and you follow where you lack.

These issues, and many more, are addressed by Craig Ponder in a much fuller and knowledgeable way. I've just described the tip of the ice berg, but in *Cracking the Apostolic and Prophetic Code*, Craig Ponder makes a forthright and valiant effort to look at the entire picture. This book definitely confronts the status quo and challenges the traditionalists, religionists, and the protective and controlling methods of some leaders. Whether you agree or disagree is not the issue. The issue is that you read it and think about it—pray about it, and let God speak to you. Draw your own conclusions so that all of us together can build a stronger and more glorious Church. A Church that will be a citadel within the Kingdom, exercising God's dominion in the workplace and marketplace. Then, instead of repelling the world, the church will once again draw the world to Him.

Cracking the Apostolic and Prophetic Code is a fascinating read. It is thought-provoking and challenging. It will definitely move you into that next place where God would have you.

Building Together With Him and You,

John P. Kelly

CEO, LEAD

Leadership Education for Apostolic Development

CEO, ICWBF

International Christian WealthBuilders™ Foundation

Ambassador Apostle, ICA

International Coalition of Apostles

ॐ ॐ

ENDORSEMENTS

ॐ ॐ

In a recent meeting with Prophet Craig Ponder, I was moved by his passion, love for Jesus, keen insight, and deep desire to serve the Body of Christ. For the past 20 years, he has faithfully served other men's ministries, learning valuable lessons, while growing in his own gifting and purpose.

This book, *Cracking the Apostolic and Prophetic Code* is written as a further gift with Craig's insights into Scripture as applied to the church, the market place and the workplace. I encourage the reader to receive this gift, with an open heart and mind; you will be blessed and strengthened in your journey.

Stan DeKoven, Ph.D., MFT
President,Vision International
Ramona, CA

This is a great ministry tool for all ministers and born again believers of the Spirit who have an apostolic call on their lives. It is easy to read and full of the true aspects of how the office of apostolic ministry can be applied in the real world, without being overcomplicated. Prophet Craig Ponder has put together his book in such a way that it can be easily and quickly accessed and digested for those who have just heard the call of the Kingdom, and for those who have been in apostolic ministry for some time. It was a pleasure to read.

Esteban Antonio
World Renowned Guitarist
Founder, White Horse Ministry International
Montreal, CANADA

As you read this book and meditate on every word, a fresh impartation is released to break poverty mindsets and create faith to possess heavens strategies for Kingdom wealth. Craig Ponder is not just speaking words but a living reality that has become a lifestyle for him. *Cracking the Apostolic and Prophetic Code* breaks bondages created by religion and tradition. The revelation in this book will set many free from traditions of men and will release you into creative thinking to access Kingdom and biblical wealth. God has given Apostle Ponder a strategy to deploy the body of Christ into all levels of business and professional spheres so that global dominance becomes a reality for the Kingdom.

Prophet Michelle McClain
Crusaders Church in Chicago, IL
IMPACT Network

This is a much needed addition to the apostolic view of marketplace ministry: in fact, I see that God has taken you into places where few have gone! I am already praising the Lord for this new book. Don't make the mistake of picking this book up if you don't have some time to spend reading and digesting its contents. That's what I did; I thought, "I will take a quick look and see what the prophet has to say." I was soon rearranging my schedule to spend more time in this revelatory book. I have been involved with the Marketplace Ministry movement for over a dozen years and yet Prophet Craig has captured the mind of God and plan of God in a way that I have not seen before. So, clear the schedule and start reading; you will soon be on your way to breaking the code in your own life, and stepping into the victory that God has designed you for!

Cracking the Apostolic and Prophetic Code is a groundbreaking book. Prophet Craig Ponder has moved into the heavenly realms to unlock the code for the Marketplace! I am very excited to see the results in my own life and in yours as a result of taking in the insights from this book. This is a book for every marketplace Apostle and Prophet in the Kingdom! And, Pastors, this one will help you to equip and release these powerful marketplace ministers into your city!"

Rich Marshall
Author of *God @ Work Volumes 1 & 2*
ROI Leadership International
San Jose, CA

I want to commend Prophet Craig Ponder for his timely new book, *Cracking the Apostolic and Prophetic Code* and highly endorse it as a cutting edge "must read." I believe that the revelation in this book birthed out of the heart of God for such a time as this, will become a powerful key in the hands of many desiring to be positioned for the wealth transference God has promised His people for ruling and reigning in the earth. As I was reading through the manuscript, I sensed a powerful apostolic and prophetic anointing. That kind of impartation is released when a man's message has also become his life.

The Word of God links believing and obeying what the true prophet says to prosperity (2 Chronicles 20:20, Ezra 6:14). Craig Ponder is an apostolic-prophet God has raised up in this generation to help prepare the way for many generations to come. Not only is *Cracking the Apostolic and Prophetic Code* full of insights and strategies, but if you will receive this book as a prophetic word from the Lord and begin to act on it, then I believe that the Spirit of Faith will rise up in you to begin to see and experience great Kingdom exploits.

Apostle Axel Sippach
President and Founder, Liaison International
Executive Director, IMPACT Network
Seaback, WA

Prophet Craig Ponder's book, *Cracking the Apostolic and Prophetic Code*, is an insightful tool for the Body of Christ. It will empower readers to impact the kingdoms of this world system by releasing apostolic and prophetic strategies for wealth transfer, spiritual authority, and Kingdom transformation.

Apostle Tom Hamon
Senior Pastor, Christian International
Family Church in Santa Rosa, FL

Cracking the Apostolic and Prophetic Code will help you shift into a fresh Kingdom dynamic; filled with freedom, empowered through purpose and overflowing with the blessings and favor of the Lord.

Apostle Jane Hamon
Senior Pastor, Christian International
Family Church in Santa Rosa, FL
Author of *The Cyrus Decree* and *The Deborah Company*

Cracking the Apostolic and Prophetic Code will awaken the spirit of the five-fold man or woman of God. It will challenge them to step into the original plan of God for His church. This book will alert you to the call of the Spirit in walking out your true destiny—whether you are an apostle, prophet, pastor, teacher, or evangelist. Anyone called to the five-fold ministry should read this book with an open heart and respond to the promptings of the Holy Spirit. The enlightening truths will take you into the next level and advance you with momentum in the call of God on your life!

Apostle Mark A. Griffo
Founder/Apostle of Glory Mountain Apostolic Base
San Marcos, CA

With profound wisdom and clarity Prophet Craig Ponder takes on issues at the crux of a major transition underway in the Body: the prophetic, apostolic, marketplace, and workplace. That he thanks his critics and enemies for the rejection that caused him to seek God more deeply, alone, underscore the value of this message. Yet, there is more, much more. Indeed, the depth of *Cracking the Apostolic and Prophetic Code* carries a rich precision and anointing that only can come from time spent in the presence of the Lord. *Cracking the Apostolic and Prophetic Code* represents a refreshing and out-of-the-box perspective that not only will mobilize, but has mapped out a pathway to unity as the Body faces the realities of understanding the times and knowing what to do. The strategic nature of this fresh message is one that should be read by every committed believer who desires to make a difference.

Morris E. Ruddick
President of Strategic Initiatives Foundation
and Ruddick International, and author of *The Daniel-Joseph Calling and God's Economy, Israel, & The Nations*
Denver, CO

Whenever God does a fresh new thing in the earth, there is always great misunderstanding and controversy. The Apostolic and Prophetic move of God is no exception. The Body of Christ needs a mature voice to arise and end the controversy and to bring understanding of what the Lord is doing in the current season. Prophet Craig Ponder has risen with great wisdom to answer this need in his book, *Cracking the Apostolic and Prophetic Code*. You will soar to new dimensions of revelation after reading this timely book. I highly recommend it to anyone wanting to experience the highest and best God has for their lives!

Barbara Wentroble
President, Founder – International Breakthrough Ministries
Author – *Prophetic Intercession; Praying with Authority; You Are Anointed; Rise to Your Destiny, Woman of God*
Coppell, TX

This is a great book for those who are looking for the right combination to opening the transference of wealth into our generation. This book is revelatory, insightful, practical, and transformational. I highly recommend both the book and the man.

Dr. Keith Johnson
TheConfidenceCoach.com
Spring Hill, FL

After reading the manuscript to *Cracking the Apostolic and Prophetic Code* I fully endorse this campaign and work. *Cracking the Apostolic & Prophetic Code* is a cutting edge, revolutionary book that is certain to transform the way the saints of God look at the five fold ministry. I believe Prophet Craig Ponder has cracked the code that will reveal what God has placed inside each reader. There is a timely refreshing that comes from reading this book that will help many frustrated saints find their part in the Kingdom of God.

Apostle Robert Summers Sr.
Authority of the Believers Ministries
Former Banking & Wall Street Vice President
Westerville, OH

Working with Craig Ponder to bring this project into print has been a delight. His transparency and forthright, "matter-of-fact" tone is refreshing in a sea of carbon-copy marketplace sound bytes. His concepts are thought-provoking and even controversial—exactly the recipe for true reformation. Read *Cracking the Apostolic and Prophetic Code* with an open mind and allow God's Spirit to speak to you. Let the Anointing of God that rests in you be released. Fulfill your destiny!

Wendy K. Walters
Palm Tree Productions
Keller, TX

ॐ ॐ

PROPHETIC WORDS

SPOKEN OVER PROPHET CRAIG A. PONDER, SR., CEA

ॐ ॐ

- ॐ Apostle John Eckhardt: Unusual Gathering Anointing coming upon you and in the days ahead you shall be able to gather many. *January 18, 2002*

- ॐ Apostle Barbara Wentroble: I see a laser like focus coming into your life, I see an increase of responsibility. The Lord wants to do something new. He wants you to be a spiritual father.I also see rank in the spirit, like as a corporal. I see the colors purple and gold and it represents royalty. I see divine connections coming, I see multiplication, and I see you as an apostle with the heart of a father and I see you bringing about radical change. *October 27, 2005 (The First Power To Get Wealth Conference)*

- ॐ Dr. Gary Greenwald: I see the favor of the Lord coming upon you and I see you taking entire teams into large arenas and shifting entire cities and business people into the Kingdom. I also see you going into churches that are on the verge of bankruptcy and you will shift them out and into new realms of prosperity. You will also be sent to kings and presidents of countries and corporations with the Word of the Lord. *April 15, 2007*

ɛ⊃ Apostle Rob DeLuca: I see you climbing to the third step of a ladder and the platform that you are now standing on is huge and you are prophesying to people, and you are throwing gold coins out into the audience, but the people are not catching them with their hands they are opening up their mouths and are swallowing the gold coins. You are a prophet of wealth. *May 9, 2007*

ɛ⊃ Apostle John Eckhardt: You and your wife are an Aquilla and Priscilla team, and you will help raise up and train the next generation of leaders. *June 30, 2007*

ɛ⊃ Prophet Michelle McClain: God sets you over nations this day and you will be known as one who roots up and tears down. *June 30, 2007*

ɛ⊃ Apostle Axel Sippach: You shall be known all over the country doing seminars: "The Prophetic in the Market Place," and you shall teach others how to prosper with the prophetic. *June 30, 2007*

ɛ⊃ Prophet Theresa Skoff: New doors have come upon you. These new doors are going to open and I really believe that you're a man that speaks with great power and great authority. I'm seeing ten doors—ten *kairos* moments, new doors, new relationships, and new opportunities. There are going to be doors in the marketplace. There are going to be kings that you're going to be sent to minister to. God, this man has been on the back burner for a long time simmering and it feels like the water is going to go out, but You're bringing him to the front and your pouring fresh water into his pot, God. And like the prophet, Father God, there is a fresh word coming out and its going to heal the body, I thank you for that, Father God. I thank you that his season has come. *August 14, 2007*

ꝏ Apostle A. Lewis Brown: You and your wife are unique and are on a different path. You are beating to a different sound. You are an anomaly, and God is not going to just use you to shift entire congregations financially and economically, but I also see you shifting entire countries and nations into new realms of wealth. *February 7, 2008*

ꝏ Apostle Axel Sippach: God is gathering friends all over the earth that He will begin to speak to regarding economic shifts, trends, investments—and you are one of those friends. *March 8, 2008*

ê Apostle Mark Kauffman: I see several things and key words that are over your lives. I see tremendous influence and tremendous favor and it is going to bring exposure. Something that has been needed within your life and ministry is exposure. The later part of 2008 is just going to be a foretaste of what God has for you, because 2009 will be a tsunami of exposure. The anointing is going to begin to increase on the both of you as you begin to move in this new season. You're going to see tremendous relationships and new doors open for you. You've been in hiding time, God told Elijah go and hide yourself, but the day came when God said go and show yourself. God says that the time has come go show yourselves, hiding time is over great exposure and many doors are about to open. *June 19, 2008*

ê Prophet Pamela Kent: Your sons shall be mighty in the Earth—you shall see your legacy go so strong across the Earth. I place the multiplication anointing upon your life and everything you touch is going to turn to gold. You will teach them how to buy property and land. You will teach the expansion of the Kingdom like never before, and I hear the Lord say that I called you because you are innocent. I hear the Lord saying that you will attack systems of men like never before, and you will stand as a General of your time, and you will cause the young generation not to back off and you will put within their spirit an ability to pursue and to overtake and recover all. *June 28, 2008*

A WORD FROM THE AUTHOR

Over the past year, as I was writing this book and receiving it's revelation, I had a visitation from four angels. In over twenty years of being saved and in the ministry, I had no previous angelic visitations. So, all I can think is that this book, its content, its information, and its revelation must be very important to God the Father. The first angel that visited me was the Angel of Revelation, the second was the Angel of Deliverance, the third was the Angel of Wealth, and the fourth was the Angel of Accuracy—"A Champion Angel," the same angel that was with David when he slew Goliath. As you read this book and begin to receive and embrace its revelation, I release these angels into your life, business, and ministry.

If you are a four-walled church leader or pastor I have one request for you. Please do not try and read this book, and then preach its revelation as your own. After you read it (or even while you are reading it), make it available to your entire congregation. Then ask the Holy Spirit to show you who the MarketPlace and Work Place Leaders are who are called to go out-side of the four walls of your church. Help raise up a team for your territory. Tell your congregation that you are looking for Kingdom Representatives to rise up and take their place, and that you welcome their feedback. Let them know you are looking forward to what they will share after they read the book.

I encourage you to let those that you identify pub-licly preach, teach, and release its revelation from the pulpit to the entire congregation. I do not encourage you to start Bible study groups around this subject.

I guarantee that if you allow those that God has al-ready placed within your sphere of influence to shift into their gifts and calling, the glory of God and the wealth of your territory (which are souls and finances) will be released to advance the Kingdom of God like never before.

Remember, priests pray and kings decree! So start declaring your rights and privileges in the Kingdom today!

Prophet Craig A. Ponder, Sr., CEA

ॐ ৫

INTRODUCTION

ॐ ৫

Cracking the Apostolic and Prophetic Code is a message to Kingdom Representatives and the next generation. Specifically, this book is written to people who are called business leaders, lay leaders, or Christian marketplace leaders. Today, it is not enough just to be a Christian in business or to be a Christian business owner. **There is a greater function for you. There is a greater anointing available to you.** This book is written to those who have been called everything BUT what Jesus called you. Ephesians 4:11 says, *"It was He who gave SOME to be apostles, SOME to be prophets..."* Men label people with every imaginable title—every title, that is, except the one that Christ has given you.

In the marketplace, there are apostles and prophets who are functioning well and fulfilling their calling. These men and women understand their anointing and are actively exercising their authority and taking dominion over their realm of influence. The inability of the *four-walled* church to recognize this authority and calling is a major reason why the transfer of wealth has yet to take place. This is why the *four-walled* church has no authority in the marketplace. Jesus released us to go **into** the world. The church will not release us to go anywhere **but** inside its own four walls.

What is the Four-walled Church?

When I speak of the *four-walled* church, I am not talking about the church established by Jesus in Matthew 16:18-19, "...*and upon this rock I will build My church; and the gates of hell shall not prevail against it. And I will give unto thee the keys of the Kingdom of Heaven: and whatsoever thou shalt bind on earth shall be bound in heaven: and whatsoever thou shalt loose on earth shall be loosed in heaven.*" The church Jesus established is a church filled with power and function. When I reference the *four-walled* church, I am speaking of church administration and church leadership that only sanctions ministry when it is carried out and contained *within* the confines of a church building. The *four walls* represent unseen barriers erected by church leaders that keep people inside, hindering them from carrying out their greater function **beyond** the church building. In the *four-walled* church, ministry that is "outside" the church's charter, bylaws, vision, or mission is discouraged—viewed as aberrant or rebellious. This keeps people from advancing the Kingdom of God in the world. This also keeps people from fulfilling their calling, reaching their destiny and carrying out the Great Commission.

This *four-walled* institution bears little resemblance to the Church that Jesus established on earth. Jesus established the church and gave us apostles, prophets, evangelists, pastors, and teachers to **equip** the **saints** to **do the work** of the ministry. If you read on in Ephesians 4, you learn that "every part (of the body) does its share," and that the purpose of the parts doing their share is to cause the "growth of the body" (Ephesians 4:16 NKJV). If the church keeps the ministry *inside* the four walls and only ministers to others already in the church, how will the Body of Christ grow? How will we exercise dominion in the earth? How will we advance the Kingdom of God and establish the authority of Christ in **every** area of society? We must first crack the Apostolic and Prophetic code — understand our role, recognize our anointing, and take our place. We must not limit ourselves to using our gifts *inside* the *four-walled* church. We must learn to exercise our gifts in the arena we were called to, fulfilling our destiny and accomplishing the purposes of God in the earth.

"To you has been entrusted the mystery of the kingdom of God (that is, the secret counsels of God which are hidden from the ungodly); but for those outside (of our circle) everything becomes a parable."

Mark 4:10,11 AMP

There are mysteries in the Kingdom. These mysteries can only be known by revelation. The church is not the Kingdom and being a church member does not automatically make you a Kingdom Representative. The church is just a part or piece of the Kingdom. The Kingdom is made up of both the Kingdom of Heaven (unseen) realm and the Kingdom of God (seen/earthly) realm.

Come with me and unlock the Apostolic and Prophetic Code. Allow the revelation of God to reveal the mysteries of the Kingdom and open doors of opportunity for you to walk in fullness, exercise dominion, and fulfill your destiny.

ℬ ℭ

CHAPTER ONE

THE THREE GATES
OF HEAVEN

ℬ ℭ

Before you can crack the Apostolic and Prophetic Code, you must first understand that there are three gates of heaven. It is through one of these gates (openings or portals) that you are granted access to the realm where God has called you to rule and reign in the earth. Revelations 5:10 says, "...*(Jesus) has made us unto our God, kings and priests: and we shall reign (rule) on the earth.*" Notice who was made to rule first? You, KING! We will cover those realms (or kingdoms) in greater detail, but before we get to those, you need to understand the three gates (openings or portals) and be aware of which gate you have been called to enter.

What is a gate? A gate is an opening, different then a door or a window. Webster's defines the word **gate** as "an opening in a wall or fence, a city, or castle entrance often with defensive structures (such as towers), a means of entrance or exit, a door, valve, or other device for controlling a passage."

In *The Prophet's Dictionary,* Dr. Paula A. Price, describes a gate as "something very important in Bible symbology." Gates were very important. They were installed at the city entrance and were also used to guard castles. The purpose of the gate was to provide a movable barrier through which people could be screened and enter the city upon permission. Ancient gates were opened in the morning and locked at night. **They were the only way to lawfully enter the city.** The guards patrolling the gates were a combination of peacekeepers and soldiers. Metaphorically, it was understood in antiquity that once a king entered a city by its gate, he had access and control of all its wealth, commerce, and resources. When he entered through the gate, he

Gates are very important in Bible symbology.

seized full authority over the land. Gates were also where business was transacted, courts were convened, and where diplomatic figures carried out political affairs.

Revelation 22:12-14 says, *"And behold, I come quickly; and my reward is with me, to give every man according as his work shall be. I am Alpha and Omega the beginning and the end, the first and the last. Blessed are they that do his commandments, that they may have right to the tree of life, and may enter in through the gates into the city."*

Genesis 24:60 says, *"And they blessed Rebekah and said to her, 'Our sister, may you increase to thousands upon thousands; may your offspring possess the gates of their enemies.'"*

"And I will give you the keys of the (gates of the)* *kingdom of heaven, and whatever you bind on earth will be bound in heaven, and whatever you loose on earth will be loosed in heaven."*

Matthew 16:19

*(author's note)

The First Gate: The Church

The first gate of heaven is the church, the *ecclesia*. But what is the church and what does the word 'church' really mean? Many believers today have been scattered from the *four-walled* church—just like the church at Jerusalem. Believers were scattered in their day because of great persecution, but today they are being scattered because of GREAT REJECTION! They are unable to find their function and have wandered away from an organized institution known as a 'church.'

My wife, Darlene, and I are a team (together, like Aquilla and Priscilla). We have been called together to impart a present day truth—to encourage, confirm, and release those believers who are scattered. In 2006 (after nineteen years of established ministry in the local *four-walled* church and in the marketplace), I (like Jesus) was called to go **outside** the *four-walled* church. I am called to gather those who are **outside** of the institution of the church. As a king, an apostle and prophet, my message (my authority), will pertain to the Kingdom that is located outside the four walls of the church.

Jesus was hidden for thirty years. But when His time came, Jesus rose up and began to do the work of His Father and the work of an apostle. In much the same way, not only have apostles and prophets been hidden, their revelation and their creativity has also been hidden—but now their time has come! Now, in our generation, they are rising up and being revealed. This does not diminish the role of pastors in any way, but it is time to clarify the function of pastors and establish what their role truly is.

For too long, the message to anyone with a heart to minister was for them to quit their secular job, enter a seminary, and go into full time 'Gospel' ministry. I am saying that it is time for man to leave this 'fool-time' ministry and join God's *true* full-time ministry. This will be a paradigm shift for five-fold ministry leaders that have been launched, but have found themselves stuck inside the boundaries of a church, or overseeing a church when they should have been in the market-place all along. They are ill placed and outside the true dominion of their calling. They have been ineffective, grown frustrated, created doctrines, and sadly, have often hindered the work of the Kingdom.

Full-time, five-fold ministers are all around us—and they are not on the payroll of any *four-walled* church. Full-time five-fold ministers who recognize that their calling, their skills, their gifts, and their vocation open up

Full-time, five-fold ministers are all around us—and they are not on the payroll of any 'four-walled' church.

countless opportunities for influence, signs and wonders, and Kingdom advancement. Now *that* is spreading the Gospel (good news). The reason why it is considered good news, is because the Kingdom is here RIGHT NOW, AMONG US—IT IS IN OUR HANDS!

When Jesus began his earthly ministry, there was an established church (the *four-walled church*) already present. The structure (or institution) was already in place. Jesus wasn't born of the household of a priest or the established ministry class. Jesus was brought to the home of a carpenter—a family in the marketplace, outside the established church. Even at the time of His birth, the church system was in place, but the system was not yet whole. Jesus *did* speak in the synagogue (as was his custom), but He *ministered and released the Kingdom of Heaven* in the street. He performed His first miracle OUTSIDE the church, met with His leaders OUTSIDE the church, and established His ministry OUTSIDE the four walls of the church. He was baptized (confirmed or set in His place) in the River Jordan OUTSIDE the four walls of the church.

So, if Jesus' revelation was for those outside the *four-walled* church, and if His message was to establish the Kingdom, and if He told us that, "greater works shall we do," then what are we waiting for?

From the moment Jesus came out of the wilderness and heard that John was cast into prison, He NEVER looked back. When He spoke, the first thing that He instructed them to do was to change their direction. He opened up the gate INTO the Kingdom of Heaven by saying, "Repent (*turn around*) the (*gate or opening to*) the Kingdom of heaven is at hand" (Matthew 4:1-17).

The Second Gate: Marketplace

So, if the first gate of heaven is the church, the second gate is the marketplace. What is the marketplace? It is every other place outside the four-walls of the church! It's the car wash, the super market, the golf course, the country club, etc. It's the entire world. Jesus said in **Mark 16:14-20,** "Go into ALL the world and preach the gospel (Kingdom message) to every creature (or every human being)."

The word "world" in Mark 16 is the Greek word *KOSMOS* **and means,** "the sum total of the material universe, the beauty in it, and the total of the persons living in the world."

The marketplace is represented by business owners and entrepreneurs. These are men and women who have a specific anointing for business, territories, and industries—and for people (souls). Marketplace apostles and prophets have an ability to attract and gather non-believers as well as believers who have been scattered. They have the ability to generate wealth and to manage their affairs and the affairs of others with great wisdom and flexibility. These men and women are not paid with a salary and they do not receive a

7

W-2 from an employer. All of their income, prosperity, wealth, and success is found within their mantles and is generated from operating within the gift or anointing that God Himself placed inside of them. For this reason, apostles and prophets must be raised up and released out of the four-walled church and into the Kingdom Of God. Then they can in turn help set others in their place through ordination—confirming others in their five-fold offices. This will in turn produce covenant or heavenly relationships.

Marketplace people must exercise an even greater measure of faith.

Salaried pastors, paid church staff members, and employees earning wages have the stability of expected income that is comforting and reliable. Unlike these men and women, marketplace people must exercise an even greater measure of faith. They must truly trust and believe in God—not only to run and manage their businesses, but also to care for and provide for the needs of their families as well.

In the *four-walled* church, preaching a bad sermon or posting low Sunday School attendance does not equate with a lower paycheck. Even in the workplace, a slow season for the company or taking a sick day does not usually affect the size of an employee's paycheck. For business owners, this is not so. Marketplace people must understand and get a revelation that they are kings. In the Old Testament, kings were types of apostles! Marketplace people must know that they are God's Kingdom Representatives, and that they have been sent into their territories, industries, and realms of influence.

The marketplace should not be confused with the workplace. The **workplace** is simply that—a place where people work. It is made up of employees—men and women whose sphere of influence is the office (store, warehouse, school, lab...) where they work. Their realm of authority is linked to their relationship with the one who signs their paycheck.

Marketplace has become a buzz word in many circles. In fact, in some circles, the word marketplace invokes great controversy. People scramble for the title, "Marketplace Apostle," and throw it around casually. In fact, many of the men and women who are trying to lead in the marketplace are not Marketplace Representatives of the Kingdom. In fact, they are instead, *ecclesia* (or *four-walled*) representatives (pastors) who have a Kingdom anointing, or I would say more of a Kingdom *burden* over a territory, but their anointing is primarily to equip the saints within the *four-walled* church to prepare them to be released in the marketplace.

This does not diminish their anointing or reduce their effectiveness in any way. When they operate inside their sphere of influence, and function in the place of dominion given to them by God, their authority is great. Because their anointing is not for the marketplace, their authority in the marketplace is weak and ineffective at best, and harmful at worst. **Kingdom anointing and Kingdom authority go hand in hand.** You MUST have the right to exercise dominion in the territory (industry, area, or realm) where you operate. For example, the Queen of England (while she may have great respect here), has no authority inside the United States. When in the U.S., she must yield to the authority of the President and the presiding government. When she tries to exercise authority outside of England (her realm, domain, territory), she finds that she has no *real (or legal)* power. An apostle (or pastor) who governs the church may have great respect in the marketplace, but is not commissioned to exercise authority or dominion in that territory (industry, realm).

Kingdom anointing and Kingdom authority go hand in hand.

Today what I find very interesting is that ten, fifteen, or even twenty years ago, these same *four-walled* church leaders or pastors told us that in order to be in full-time ministry or have a "real" ministry (like theirs), we had to quit our jobs or sell our businesses. Now that our day for the marketplace and the Kingdom of Heaven is at (or in) our hand to begin to rule and reign, these same *four-walled* church leaders are trying to step outside their arena (the *four-walled* church) and do what they are not called to do!

This is why it is vital that we raise up and release spiritual sons and daughters into the Kingdom of God, into the marketplace, and begin preparing the next generation. As apostles and prophets it is our job to raise them up and release them, and that is not the job or function of a pastor. Raising up and releasing is the function of apostles and prophets!

I want to be clear, one "type" of apostle or prophet is not greater than any other "type." It doesn't matter if you are called as an apostle or prophet in the *four-walled* church, in the marketplace, or in the work-place—one is not greater or better than the others! Every apostolic and prophetic leader is called to a specific place, a specific people, and a specific time! I believe that any *four-walled* church leader, pastor, or pulpit minister that doesn't fully embrace this, and who doesn't get delivered from a spirit of pride, a spirit of elitism, and the spirit of religion, is headed for a great fall!

Let me make a bold statement—if you feel called to own or start a business, or you are an entrepreneur, a sales person, or an individual paid on a 1099, I don't believe that it is possible for you to fulfill this role on behalf of the Kingdom of God, and not be either an apostle or a prophet! Am I saying then that every person that is in the marketplace is either an apostle or prophet? YES, YES and YES! Why? Because if it is your calling to be in the marketplace, you are a direct gate (opening) for heaven! Just like in Jesus' day, when Jesus asked His disciples, "whom do men say that I, the Son of Man am?" Peter was the only one to speak up, because of his revelation. Jesus then boldly stated, "that flesh and blood has not revealed this to you, but My father which was in heaven: and upon this rock (revelation) I will build my church, and the gates of hell shall not prevail against it (you and your business). And I will give you (Peter) the keys of the Kingdom *(gates)* of heaven" (Matthew 16:19).

In other words, YOU will be His GATE (His opening) into the marketplace. This is what will give you legal access to enter into your territory, city, or region and begin to rule and reign. Who was Peter? Was he a priest? A rabbi? A church leader? No. He was just like you and me. Peter was a fisherman—an entrepreneur of his day.

The moment you get the revelation that the Kingdom of Heaven is IN YOU (Luke 17:21), you WILL BECOME A GATE (OPENING or PORTAL) OF HEAVEN into your territory and society! In Psalms 115:16 it says, *"The heaven, even the heavens, are the LORD's: but the earth hath he given to the children of men."* My question to you is is this—"What are you going to do with the piece of earth (territory or region) that God has GIVEN YOU to rule and reign in?"

The Third Gate: Workplace

The third gate to access heaven is the workplace. I have already defined that there is a difference between the marketplace and the workplace. The marketplace is the realm of business—comprised of business men and business women, entrepreneurs with multiple streams of income, and who possess a wide range of influence, authority, and power.

There are influential men, *four-walled* church leaders (pastors), and entire groups and networks that are now saying that *everything* is workplace—that there is no more marketplace. Let me STOP HERE and make a bold statement—these people are either deceived or they are operating out of ignorance! In the last twenty-five years I have NEVER worked for anyone else. I have not been paid W-2 wages, or received any type of a salary which would place me in the category of the workplace. Again, one is not better then the other, but we must know our place in the Kingdom if we are going to be effective in carrying out our assignment.

We must know our place in the Kingdom if we are going to be effective in carrying out our assignment.

As a marketplace Kingdom Representative, I have FULL GOVERNMENTAL AUTHORITY along with the ABILITY to create UNLIMITED WEALTH! No one can tell me what I can and can not do. I decide when to work, how long to work, and what work I want to accomplish. If you are in the workplace, this simply means that you work for someone other than yourself. There are certain limitations placed on you "governmentally." It means that you are accountable to a boss, supervisor, board, or overseer that tells you what to do, and when to do it.

I believe that there is a major difference between the marketplace and the workplace. I believe that everyone who feels called into business by God is either an apostle or a prophet! In the workplace you can still be apostolic or prophetic. But, unless you are the CEO, the president, a corporate officer, or other high ranking executive employee (that either owns a piece of the company or has unlimited income options), you cannot be a workplace apostle or prophet. You can not rule over something that is not yours!

You cannot rule over something that is not yours!

The workplace is an important realm, and should not be left out of the equation. Here too, is another vital element of society that MUST function OUTSIDE of the *four-walled* church to maintain a viable culture. The workplace is made up of the men and women who program computers, maintain equipment, work in retail, serve in restaurants and hotels, etc. They may be doctors, lawyers, teachers, administrators, or executives in corporate America. Where would society be if every one of them felt that the only way to serve God was to quit their job and go into full time ministry? The church should be strengthening this segment of society and encouraging them to exercise dominion in their sphere—their authorized territory.

When people in the workplace learn how to take their territory in the industry (realm) that they have been called to, and begin to walk in the dominion of God, amazing opportunities to share the Kingdom of God are presented. Sadly, these men and women often neglect their calling, blithely unaware that they have an important role to play outside their local *four-walled* church. They often separate their life into "sacred" and "secular." They view their work as employment rather than as ministry. They have been taught that their ministry is being *just* a deacon, usher, greeter, Sunday school teacher or a children's church worker—never understanding that the workplace is their true place of function, authority, and calling.

I want to encourage you to get a revelation on why you get up and go to work on Monday morning, and understand how valuable you are to God! You are a gate to release His glory, love, power, expressions, and deliverance into the lives of people that the altar team just can't reach. You are not there to preach to, proselytize, or to pray with people during company hours, or on your employer's dime! You are there to let people see that the Kingdom of Heaven is at hand in your life, and through a spirit of excellence and example, the world will begin to approach you. **As you build trust and relationship, God Himself will make a way for them to approach you.** Then, as the Holy Spirit makes opportunities during your lunch break, after work in the evenings, and other times, rise up and allow God to bless people through YOUR (workplace) ministry.

You are a gate to release God's glory.

Many who are in the workplace today are gaining valuable experience, receiving training, and gathering influence that they will need in the days ahead. These people are poised to make a shift and enter into the marketplace as God's chosen Kingdom Representatives with a greater authority and momentum. These people will learn from the mistakes of others and avoid the financial setbacks that many of us have made as pioneers in the marketplace. We have blazed the trail and cleared a path for the future generations to advance and progress with miraculous strength.

SUMMARY POINTS

- ◯ Before you can crack the Apostolic and Pro-phetic Code, you must first understand the three gates of heaven.

- ◯ Each of these gates represents a sphere of au-thority on the earth, and each sphere is cre-ated with a unique function. All three spheres must interact with one another, but they each operate in a different way and have a different job to do.

- ◯ In the church established by Jesus, all three spheres are enveloped by His church. They are not separate from His church—all are part of His Body and therefore connected in relation-ship. Romans 12:4-6 says, *"For as we have many members in one body, and all members have not the same office: So we, being many, are one body in Christ, and every one members one of another. Having then gifts differing accord-ing to the grace that is given to us, whether prophecy, let us prophesy according to the pro-portion of faith."*

- ◯ In this book, I am separating the spheres (church, marketplace, and workplace) for the purpose of clarity. By defining each sphere, it is easier to see how people function in the earth.

17

The current separation of the 'sacred' vs. the 'secular' limits the effectiveness of ministry in any realm outside the *four-walled* church.

○ Each gate (or sphere) is part of the Body of Christ. Each gate needs apostles and prophets established in their authority and functioning in their roles to take dominion and fulfill the purpose of God in the earth.

○ Jesus said in Luke 11:49, "...*I will send them prophets and apostles, and some of them they shall slay and persecute.*"

Gate One: The Church

When I use the term "church" in this book, I am speaking about the actual *four-walled* institution. It is a place where men and women are to be equipped with wisdom, knowledge, and understanding of God's Word. It is a place where they are to be trained, raised up, and released to function—primarily *within* the *four-walled church* in whatever leadership capacity that God has called them to or that the *ecclesia* leaders need them to function in, using their gifts, calling, or talents.

Gate Two: The Marketplace

This is the arena of business owners and entrepreneurs who are really kings—Kingdom Representatives who are also apostles and prophets. This is a place where men and women are effective in creating wealth and exercise great influence over society. **Lost people are easily reached by those with the ability to touch them, solve their problems, demonstrate love in action, operate in strong deliverance, and perform signs and wonders.**

I believe that this is the place that Jesus was talking about in Acts 1:8 when He said, *"But ye shall receive power, after that the Holy Ghost is come upon you: and ye shall be witnesses unto me both in Jerusalem, and in all Judaea, and in Samaria, and unto the uttermost part of the earth."* I also think this is what is referred to in Mark 16:15-20 when He said, *"Go ye into all the world, and preach the gospel to every creature. He that believeth and is baptized shall be saved; but he that believeth not shall be damned. And these signs shall follow them that believe; In My Name shall they cast out devils; they shall speak with new tongues; They shall take up serpents; and if they drink any deadly thing, it shall not hurt them; they shall lay hands on the sick, and they shall recover. So then after the Lord had spoken unto them, He was received up into heaven, and sat on the right hand of God. And they went forth, and preached everywhere, the Lord working with them, and confirming the word with signs following."* Amen.

Gate Three: The Workplace

This is the arena of employees and the places where they work. Here too, men and women can be very effective in reaching the lost. **This is where lost people are.** Most large corporations are run by powerful men and women with an executive management team that the *four-walled* church leadership would never be able to reach or even have access to. Those operating in the realm of the workplace (as employees) can and will be used by God to speak and demonstrate His miraculous signs and wonders in the lives of those they work with and for.

Workplace people touch corporations through their influence. In some cases, the powerful individuals of society that own or manage these corporations may only be reached by those in the workplace. There may never be an opportunity for them to be touched by the *four-walled* church or by an evangelistic team, or even by those that are in the marketplace. **When people recognize their authority and take dominion, operate in their gifts and calling, and use them to change lives, real ministry occurs.** The Kingdom of God expands and then, and only then, *"...the saints of the most High shall take the kingdom, and possess the kingdom for ever; even forever and ever. Until the Ancient of Days came, and judgment was given to the saints of the most High; and the time came that the saints possessed the kingdom.*

> *Workplace people touch corporations through their influence.*

And the kingdom and dominion, and the greatness of the kingdom under the whole heaven, shall be given to the people of the saints of the most High, whose kingdom is an everlasting kingdom, and all dominions shall serve and obey Him" (Daniel 7:18, 22 & 27).

Only then can Jesus come back to redeem His bride (us), because we have made our enemy our footstool, and he (Satan) is under our feet (Luke 20:43)!

THE THREE GATES OF HELL

ॐ ☙

We have discussed the three gates of Heaven, the Ecclesia (church), the Marketplace, and the Workplace. But to fully understand the Apostolic and Prophetic Code, you must also comprehend the power posed by the three gates (or strongholds) of Hell. These gates are a blockade to the fulfillment of your destiny. They are; Religion, Tradition, and Racism. These gates represent mindsets and strongholds that grip the minds of men and women—especially those that have been in the *four-walled* church. These strongholds can keep them from realizing their dreams, their destiny, and their calling. The influence of these three gates of hell must be dealt with in order to operate FULLY in the Kingdom of God. You must be free from their bondage and control before you can truly exercise dominion and begin to rule and reign.

Always remember that Satan is a copy cat or an imitator of God. God is a creator. Satan is not a creator, and thus has never produced anything new. Instead, he counterfeits God's methods, strategies, or plans. So, if God has 3 gates, then Satan will have 3 gates. Satan's tendency to counterfeit the things of God is why it is so important for you to know God's word and will for your life. Matthew 22:29 says, *"You do err, not knowing the scriptures, nor the power of God."*

Many Christians deny the possibility that a stronghold could affect them. It is important that you understand the reality of these strongholds, and so before we cover the first gate, let's first take a look at what a mindset and a stronghold really are.

Mindsets and Strongholds

Apostle John Eckhardt, in *The Dictionary of the Apostolic* (page 204), defines a mindset in this way. Mindset: a set way of thinking, whether good or bad. Mindsets can either advance or hinder the plans and purposes of God for one's life. A mindset can be a stronghold that opposes the truth of God. Apostle Eckhardt defines strongholds for us (page 208). Strongholds: (2 Corinthians 10:4) from the Greek word, *OCHUROMA*, meaning to fortify through the idea of holding safely; a castle of fortification. Stronghold also means an argument. Strongholds can be the arguments that men and women have, resisting the truth. These arguments are inspired by demons that prevent men and women from accepting the truth.

The weapons of the apostolic ministry are mighty through God to the pulling down of these strongholds. Mindsets that resist the truth are challenged through the teaching and preaching of an apostle. Apostolic preaching is a weapon against the imaginations, reasonings, speculations, arguments, knowledge, and thoughts that are fortresses and strongholds that Satan builds in the minds of men and women to keep them from the knowledge (know-how) of God.

For example, a common mindset among *four-walled* church leaders is that the ONLY WAY to be in full time ministry, is for a person to quit their full time "secular" job or business, go through seminary, and then start (or work for) a church. This is a lie. We have lost many leaders, families, and great men and women of God because of this mindset. The result of this error has caused many to be out of order in their lives, their calling, and even their finances—unknowingly forsaking the will of God. Understand that there is nothing wrong with seminary. If you are called to operate inside the *four-walled* church, then seminary is a proper training ground to prepare you for that assignment. However, if you are called to operate inside the marketplace, seminary training will not equip you for that assignment. You need business training and experience for that. Thank God for deliverance! The truth in this book will set you free. Once free, you can join me to help set others free.

Consider this, Jesus never went to seminary. His apostles never went to seminary. But, He did spend three and a half years pouring into them and when they were ready, He called them, empowered them, identified them as apostles, and sent them out (Matthew 10). Then He told them to go and tarry until they would be endued (filled) with power from on high (Acts 1:8). After this He gave gifts to men—the same five-fold gifts (offices or mantles) that He had. These were the same gifts that He operated in while He was here on earth (Ephesians 4:8-16). Remember, Jesus was talking to marketplace leaders and Kingdom representatives.

Let me ask you a question. Have you ever thought that you were right about something, only to find out later that you were wrong? If you didn't admit it, and confess this to anyone, you were operating from a mindset—a stronghold!

The First Gate of Hell: Religion

Religion will always say "WE DON'T DO THAT!"

Webster's Dictionary defines religion as: commitment or devotion to religious faith or observance; a personal set of beliefs; an institutionalized system of religious attitudes, beliefs, and practices; scrupulous conformity to a cause, principle, or system of beliefs held to with ardor and faith.

In the Greek, the word for religion is *THREESKIA* meaning religious worship, especially external; that which consists in ceremonies (*from Thayer's Greek Lexicon, Electronic Database. Copyright © 2000, 2003 by BibleSoft, Inc. All rights reserved*). Rather than being in a relationship with God, the focus of religion is on the external—an act or ceremony, and points more to man than it does to Christ. People locked in a religious mindset adopt a set of unchangeable rules, patterns, and systems. The word of the appointed leader is accepted as higher than Scripture. This is illustrated by the Mormon faith, where the "revelation" to Joseph Smith supercedes the Scripture. Another example is the "infallibility" of the Pope—declaring Papal Law to have the ability to override the Word of God. Regardless of the times, seasons, or changes,

A religious mindset keeps people from adjusting their beliefs.

in fact, even when it contradicts the very Word of God, a religious mindset (stronghold) keeps people from adjusting their beliefs—from accepting Truth. They will follow the religious doctrine and religious leaders blindly, never searching for themselves. Extremist groups all over the world are built and maintained by the power exerted over followers by a religious stronghold.

When Jesus came out of the wilderness, He immediately said, "Repent, and follow Me." They could not do this. Why? Because they could not accept that He was the Messiah. They could not entertain the idea that this carpenter's son was the fulfillment of prophesy, the hoped for Messiah. In James 1:26-27 we learn that we deceive ourselves by THINKING we are religious. This is vain and unacceptable to God. The context of these verses is that we must be doers of the Word (and not just hearers). Religious practices and traditions are hollow and empty without obedience to the pure Word of God.

Know this also, that in the last days perilous times shall come. For men shall be lovers of their own selves, covetous, boasters, proud, blasphemers, disobedient to parents, unthankful, unholy, without natural affection, trucebreakers, false accusers, incontinent, fierce, despisers of those that are good, traitors, heady, highminded, lovers of pleasures more than lovers of God;

Having a form of godliness,
but denying the power thereof:
from such turn away.

2 Timothy 3:1-5 KJV

Religion is a stronghold made up of a set of beliefs and practices. It is comprised of "do's" and "don'ts" fashioned by men and adopted by those they can persuade to follow them. Religion can take on many, many forms; secularism, humanism, cults, etc. You can see in the Bible passage above that even Christianity can be reduced to mere religion; holding to a form of godliness that is void of power and bereft of God's authority.

Hell is filled with men and women who had "religion."

Hell is filled with men and women who had "religion." In fact, Satan loves to use religion to ensnare the souls of men and keep them from tasting and experiencing the power of the Kingdom of Heaven. There is no door to Heaven other than Jesus. In John 14:6 Jesus says, *"I am the way, the truth, and the life: no man cometh unto the Father, but by me."* Only salvation by grace, made possible by the atoning blood of Jesus grants you access

29

to the throne. **Religion is not a substitute for the cross.** Neither will religion recognize or release you to fulfill your purpose. Religion was not ready to accept Jesus Christ, and will NEVER be ready to release you to fulfill your destiny. **Religion is based on hierarchy and power.** You completing your assignment and fulfilling your purpose just isn't on the agenda.

You have been called by God. Your authority has been given to you by God—not by any form of religion or organization. You may have ordination papers or a license that legally identifies you as a minister. This has been given to you by a man or an organization. But what that paper actually does, is publicly recognize and confirm what the man (or organization) granting the ordination already sees placed in you by God Himself! Those papers don't determine your purpose. They don't control or direct you, and they especially don't make you who you are in Christ. That doesn't mean that ordination (or being commissioned) is not important. What I am saying is that an ordination or license is a validation of God's gifts at work, being expressed through your life. The ordination is recognition (by man) of God's calling on you. Many ordained or licensed individuals are NOT fulfilling their calling and NOT exercising God's purpose. An ordination alone is not enough to make you a leader. And, not having an ordination is not enough to keep you from leading. You are who you are. You are what God has called you to be.

Religion shuns the prophetic and disdains the apostolic. When you become aware of your calling and begin to reach for your destiny, organized religion is the first to say, "Don't do that." Religion is restrictive and thrives on legalism, hierarchy, and oppression. Religion is a stronghold that places limitations on faith and ignores the ability of individuals to hear the voice of God without a mediator. Unlike organized religion, the apostolic and the prophetic do not put a lot of emphasis on man (themselves) or organizations (their churches or ministries). Instead, apostolic and prophetic leaders concentrate on pouring into their spiritual sons and daughters—raising up the next generation of leaders. Apostles and prophets focus on YOU and what God has called YOU to do in the Kingdom.

Religion Tears the Fabric of Families

My wife and I were involved in a church where we were key leaders for five years. During that time, I observed that I never saw any of the members out in the city enjoying their lives. We are only about fifteen minutes from the ocean, yet I never saw (or heard about) any of them taking the time to enjoy the beach. They didn't enjoy the city, didn't take in movies, and never had the time or freedom to just hang out and have fun. Why? The pastor and church leaders never stood in the pulpit and told them they couldn't have fun or go to the movies. But they also didn't encourage them to do it either. Missing church functions to be with family was looked at as a lack of commitment, or a poor reflection on your choice of priorities. Deuteronomy 8:1 tells us that we should live, we should multiply, and we should go out and possess the land.

My wife and I first got involved with the leadership of this church in 2002. Our family had always traveled, but once we became a part of the leadership, we were immediately discouraged from traveling. When we did, we felt condemned. We needed permission to leave for vacation or go on weekend trips together. They would even make us submit the request in writing. They would say things to me like, "Didn't you just go somewhere?" And I'd say, "Yeah."

Listen, I believe in accountability and submission, but one of the advantages of the apostolic and prophetic is that we operate in teams. The work of the ministry is not solely dependent on any one individual. Our family likes to travel. We work hard and we like to take time away to refresh and restore our relationship with God and with each other. We are married and in love. Spontaneity in our relationship is a blessing. It's healthy, it's good, and it's normal. It was not reasonable for us to give a two or a three week notice prior to an excursion. But, instead of supporting how we chose to strengthen our family unit, we were discouraged from this. Although I believe the leaders were well-intentioned, trying to "build church," they were operating from a mindset of control, and it was not healthy.

I want to share an example that illustrates the destructive force of a religious stronghold. One New Year's Eve, our family decided that instead of going to church to bring in the New Year, we wanted to go hang out at a hotel in La Jolla, CA. We just wanted to be together, laugh, and watch old movies. I wasn't on the church's schedule to do anything, and my family really wanted to just spend a little time together. That evening while we were on the freeway driving to the hotel, the pastor called me and said, "Hey, nobody knows where you're at. Nobody knows what's going on. Are you going to be at church tonight?" I had to tell him, "No, as a matter of fact my family and I are in the car. We've got a hotel room and we're going to go hang out and have fun together. If you want me to turn the car around and come to church, I will, but I'll lose my reservation."

As a Christian and as human beings there was nothing wrong with what we were doing. In fact, I want to encourage you that if you're not enjoying life, or if you find that you are spending little time with your family and more time at church, you need to re-think some things. Many people perform more acts of service for their local church than they do for their immediate family. This is out of balance. Religious spirits will keep you tied to so many commitments that your family relationships begin to break down—this is not God's order. Your family is your stewardship. God is a God of relationships, He loves families, and His order strengthens and builds families. I want to encourage you to take some money, take some time, and spend it with your wife, spend it with your children, spend it refreshing, relaxing, and rebuilding. GO OUT AND HAVE SOME FUN! The control of religion will quench your joy and keep you from enjoying the very things God gave you dominion over.

Your family is yours to steward over, as surely as your finances.

The scripture says in Romans 14:17, *"For the kingdom of God is not meat and drink; but righteousness, and peace, and joy in the Holy Ghost."* Job 36:11 says, *"If they obey and serve him, they shall spend their days in prosperity, and their years in pleasure."* The divorce rate within the church should be very small. Adultery within the church should be a rare occurrence. Instead, divorce and infidelity equals that of the population of unbelievers. Why is this? If we would spend more time tending and building our families, and less time at mid-week meetings and weekend seminars, perhaps this would change.

Recently I heard Apostle John Eckhardt of Crusaders Church of Chicago, Illinois make a statement. He realized that his church leaders and congregation were spending too much time at church. To remedy this, they decided to take an entire month off one summer, and told the people to just mail their tithes and offerings in to the church office, take time off to rest and regenerate. Sound good? Well, the people did not know how to function. They didn't know how to have fun without coming to church. People were literally calling the church and asking what they were supposed to do. Thank God for his holy apostles or apostolic leaders who are over churches and who are sensitive to what the people of God need in this hour to stay refreshed and encouraged.

Root Spirits of Religion

One of the spirits at the root of religion is murder. Webster's defines murder as: the crime of unlawfully killing a person, especially with malice; a forethought of something very difficult or dangerous, something outrageous or blameworthy; to kill (a human being) unlawfully and with premeditated malice, to slaughter wantonly, to put an end to, to defeat badly.

The other spirit at the root of religion is control. Control is defined as this: to exercise restraining or directing influence over; to regulate—(which is to) govern or direct according to rule; to bring under the control of law or constituted authority; to make regulations for or concerning, to bring order, method, or uniformity to; to regulate one's habits; to fix or adjust the time, amount, degree, or rate of; to regulate the pressure of; to have power over, to rule—(which are the) laws or regulations prescribed by the founder of a religious order for observance by its members; an accepted procedure, custom, or habit; a personality or spirit believed to actuate the utterances or performances of a spiritualist medium inclined to exercise arbitrary and overbearing control over others.

Look what happened between Jesus and the *four-walled* church leaders of His day. They were waiting for the coming Messiah, the One who would deliver them. They had a special seat or place reserved for Him in the synagogue for Him to sit when He showed up. Let's look at Luke 4:16-30.

And He came to Nazareth, where He had been brought up: and, as His custom was, He went into the synagogue (four-walled church) on the Sabbath day, and stood up for to read. And there was delivered unto Him the book of the prophet Esaias. And when He had opened the book, He found the place where it was written, "The Spirit of the Lord is upon Me, because He hath anointed Me to preach the gospel to the poor; He hath sent Me to heal the brokenhearted, to preach deliverance to the captives, and recovering of sight to the blind, to set at liberty them that are bruised, To preach the acceptable year of the Lord."

And He closed the book, and He gave it again to the minister, and sat down. And the eyes of all them that were in the synagogue were fastened on Him. And He began to say unto them, "This day is this scripture fulfilled in your ears."

And all bare Him witness, and wondered at the gracious words which proceeded out of His mouth. And they said, "Is not this Joseph's son?"

And He said unto them, "Ye will surely say unto Me this proverb, 'Physician, heal thyself: whatsoever we have heard done in Capernaum, do also here in thy country.'"

And He said, "Verily I say unto you,

No prophet is accepted in his own country. But I tell you of a truth, many widows were in Israel in the days of Elias, when the heaven was shut up three years and six months, when great famine was throughout all the land; But unto none of them was Elias sent, save unto Sarepta, a city of Sidon, unto a woman that was a widow. And many lepers were in Israel in the time of Eliseus the prophet; and none of them was cleansed, saving Naaman the Syrian."

And all they (religious) in the synagogue, when they (religious) heard these things, were filled with wrath (anger and murder), And rose up, and thrust Him out of the city, and led Him unto the brow of the hill whereon their city was built, that they might cast Him down headlong (or murder Him). But He, passing through the midst of them, went his way.

Take a look at what Jesus said in Luke 20:45-47, *"Then in the audience of all the people He said unto his disciples, 'Beware of the scribes, which desire to walk in long robes, and love greetings in the markets, and the highest seats in the synagogues, and the chief rooms at feasts; Which devour widows' houses, and for a show make long prayers: the same shall receive greater damnation.'"*

I believe that religion is probably the most powerful evil demon spirit of Satan. Oh yes, not only is it evil and of Satan, but it is also a DEMON! It is a murdering spirit and its main purpose is to destroy. It wants to destroy you, destroy the (new) move(s) of God, and destroy the people of God on the earth. Religion's main practice (the way it exerts its rule and operates) is control. Religion seeks to control others by binding them to a lot of rules and rituals. In this way, there is a form of godliness (which keeps you believing it is right and righteous) but God's power is denied (see 2 Timothy 3:5).

The Second Gate of Hell: Tradition

Tradition says, "WE DON'T DO IT THAT WAY!"

Webster's Dictionary defines tradition as: an inherited, established, or customary pattern of thought, action, or behavior (as a religious practice or a social custom); a belief, or story, or a body of beliefs or stories, relating to the past that are commonly accepted as historical though not verifiable. I believe that tradition can also be defined as cultural continuity in social attitudes, customs, and institutions. It is also a characteristic manner, method, or style.

Apostle John Eckhardt, in *The Dictionary of the Apostolic* (page 297) defines tradition as: (Matthew 15:6) the handling down of statements, beliefs, legends, customs, etc. from generation to generation by word of mouth or by practice. I want to clearly state that some traditions (but not all) can make the Word of God of none effect. This happens when tradition is placed in authority above the Word of God. Only traditions that are filled with life and strengthen your relationship with Jesus, your family, and your friends are worth continuing.

Jesus confronted the dead traditions of His day. When Jesus began His ministry, He broke all tradition—how He started it, where He started it, and who He started it with. Have you ever wondered or thought about WHY Jesus was born in a manger (common place) and not in an inn or hotel, or at least in a church? I believe this was so that no man, no company or church (religious group) could take the credit. He was literally born outside of tradition and religion! Praise God!

I believe the number one tradition demonstrated by Christians is the practice to pray about everything. I know, I can hear you asking, "What's wrong with that?" Listen, when I hear a Christian say, "Let me pray about it," I understand that this is an auto-response that means, "I need time to think up an excuse." Have you ever really met a Christian that came back from "praying about it" with deep answers, Holy Spirit input, and a firm resolve? Mostly, this is used to avoid committing to something. When Peter needed money to pay taxes, Jesus didn't tell him to go and pray about it, He said, *"Go down to the sea with a hook (what you are good at or already know how to do) and the first fish that you catch, open up his mouth and you will find a coin. Use that to go and pay both of our taxes"* (Matthew 17:27). In other words, go and do something about it.

I want to encourage husbands and wives not to be bound by dead traditions in your marriage. Avoid the boring and routine in your love life and in your romance to one another. Stay fresh, young, and spontaneous with one another. This will DEFEAT the spirit of divorce! My wife and I go out dancing, to jazz concerts, to comedy shows, and for mini get-a-ways, and they are not all Christian-based. We go out and show the world how Kingdom couples live and have fun! Marriage is the greatest covenant on earth between two individuals, it should never be made stale by dead traditions.

A Bold Apostolic Statement

Right now I want to do two things—first, GET YOUR ATTENTION, and second, GET YOU DELIVERED! If you are bound by religion and tradition, I want you to be able to repent and turn toward the Kingdom of

Heaven. Okay, here's the bold statement—there is NO DIFFERENCE between a pimp, a master, (or plantation/slave owner), and a pastor (or *four-walled* church leader) that has a religious spirit or who is ruled by religion. Even as I type this, I can literally feel some of you in my spirit, disagreeing or arguing with that statement. But before you close the book, remember what a stronghold is—an argument that resists the truth. Let me reveal the comparison between the three and the way they operate, and then you can make up your mind if the assessment is legitimate.

A pimp rules by fear, intimidation, a sense of false love, often coupled with a fathering or covering nature. Pimps prey on people that are in desperate circumstances, have strained relationships with their immediate family, and who are away from their normal environment.

A pimp rules by fear.

A master rules by control.

A master (or plantation/slave owner) rules by legal control. He takes your rights away, immediately divides slaves from their family and positions them based on his needs. He sets one in the house because they look more acceptable. He places another in the field and establishes a hierarchy, making slaves believe that one

A pastor...

position is better than another. A master gives slaves a false belief that he cares about them and this is the reason why he provided them with a roof over their head. (When, in fact, all his "benevolence" serves his own purpose to keep his plantation well supplied with laborers). Slaves were kept uneducated, ignorant, and illiterate. If a master could control the information a slave had access to, then the master could maintain control of the slave's future and purpose. He could limit his imagination, cut off his opportunities, and keep him bound forever.

Consider this, even after slavery was abolished, many of the freed slaves remained with their masters, working for them as share croppers. Why? Because the control over them was so established that legal freedom was not enough to crush the stronghold that had taken root in their minds.

Legal freedom is not enough to crush a stronghold that has taken root in your mind.

Recently I heard Apostle Axel Sippach, Founder and President of Liaison International and Executive Director of IMPACT Network, make this statement, "The church is supposed to be a family that produces servants who are sons and daughters of the Almighty

God. Sometimes it looks as if the church is just creating church members or servants that serve the master (pastor) of a plantation!" We are the church—not a plantation! Pastors and leaders are not to be pimps or masters, "placing" people within their ministries for their own benefit, their own comfort, or to satisfy their own ego. Pastors are supposed to be servants and shepherds—equipping, training, and RELEASING people so that they can fulfill their destiny, their purpose, and complete their assignment.

Jesus exposed the character and behavior of those who make the commandment (Word) of God of no effect by the tradition of men. Jesus identified this as hypocrisy. For those who claim to honor God with their mouths, but their hearts are far from Him, all their worship (service, works, etc.) is done in vain (Matthew 15:6-9).

An Apostolic View of Tradition

Apostles confront traditions that hinder or hold the church back from obeying the Word of God. Please understand, some traditions are good and bear fruit. Traditions such as praying for the sick, laying on of hands, anointing with oil, taking communion, baptism... these are all biblical traditions that are valuable and should remain. These traditions will continue from generation to generation. Apostles must uphold and defend these traditions while rejecting the traditions of men (2 Thessalonians 2:15).

Tradition is another stronghold that hinders people from obtaining their destiny and fulfilling their calling. Tradition continues a pattern of beliefs or a way of doing things from generation to generation. Tradition says, "We don't do it that way." Even if a new way is better, produces more fruit, is effective and more economical. Any time you do something new or go a new direction it is an apostolic function. If you are thinking or acting "out-of-the-box," if you are breaking new ground or taking new territory, tradition is your enemy. Any time you challenge set patterns, established systems, protocols or rules, tradition will quickly rise up to quench your "rebellion."

Mark 7:13 NKJV chastises men for this, *"making the word of God of no effect through your tradition which you have handed down. And many such things you do."* In this same chapter, Jesus scolds the hypocrites who nullify the Word of God in favor of their own traditions.

These people honor me with their lips, but their hearts are far from me. They worship me in vain; their teachings are but rules taught by men. You have let go of the commands of God and are holding on to the traditions of men.

Mark 7:6-8 NIV

Tradition, like religion is a stronghold. It is a mindset that locks people into a paradigm and causes them to blindly follow the routines and customs of the past. It sets itself above the authority of Christ and the Word of God, therefore nullifying your right to live in the Kingdom of God and take advantage of all of its benefits, rights, and privileges!

Yielding to the traditions of men prevents you from taking responsibility for your own destiny. It is more convenient to follow a set of rules than it is to discover the will of God for your own life. Tradition places limitations around you and is the root of all comfort zones. Tradition paralyzes the anointing, the prophetic, and the apostolic which are the foundations of the New Testament church. Tradition is a yolk that will keep you in step with religion and unable to pursue your destiny. Tradition will keep you locked outside of the Kingdom of God even though it is already inside of you (Luke 17:21).

Yielding to the traditions of men prevents you from taking responsibility for your own destiny.

The Third Gate of Hell: Racism

Racism says, "YOU ARE NOT QUALIFIED TO DO IT!"

The spirit of racism measures you—and you will never measure up. You will always be either too much of this or not enough of that! In other words, no matter your anointing, your gifting, or your experience you will always be the wrong person for the job. The Spirit of God will not tolerate racism. Genesis 1:26-28 says, *"And God said, 'Let us make man in Our image, after Our likeness: and let them have dominion over the fish of the sea, and over the fowl of the air, and over the cattle, and over all the earth, and over every creeping thing that creepeth upon the earth.' So God created man in His own image, in the image of God created He him; male and female created He them. And God blessed them, and God said unto them, 'Be fruitful, and multiply, and replenish the earth, and subdue it: and have dominion over the fish of the sea, and over the fowl of the air, and over every living thing that moves upon the earth.'"*

The spirit of racism measures you—and you will never measure up.

All of us are created in God's image and God's likeness—racism expressed toward you is racism expressed toward God Himself!

When we are born again, we accept Jesus Christ into our hearts and confess Him as the Lord and Savior of our lives and the ruler of our souls. At the time of our salvation, God "re-genes" us back to our original beginning in Him. He takes us to a time before we had color on our skin, before we had gender, even before our nationality was determined. He bypasses all flesh, all dysfunctions, any generational or hereditary curses, and takes us back to when we were just spirit! Salvation is the greatest liberator, the greatest equalizer of mankind. In Him we are all heirs and joint heirs with Jesus. **When you become a citizen of the Kingdom of Heaven, you obtain all the rights and privileges of that citizenship.** God created you not OUT OF His image, but IN His IMAGE!

Webster's Dictionary defines racism as: a belief that race is the primary determinant of human traits and capacities. I offer that racism is a mindset that racial differences produce an inherent superiority of one particular race over another. This mindset creates racial prejudice or discrimination. This evil demon spirit comes directly from its father—Satan himself. Remember, Satan said that he would be like God and rise above Him. He was convincing enough that he was able to deceive a third of the angels—beings who were created for God's pleasure and knew Him intimately. If he could deceive angels, what makes us think he cannot deceive us? This is the same old trick that he used on Adam and Eve when he said (Genesis 3:1-6) that if they ate of the tree that they would not die, after all weren't they just like God? Wasn't God trying to hide something or protect his superiority by forbidding them access to that tree? Guess what? Adam and Eve were already like God, they were created in His image—and so are you! Satan constantly tries to put doubt in your mind about WHOSE you are and WHO you are.

Identity Crisis

A large problem in the Body of Christ is rooted in identity issues. Insecurity, self-doubt, self-pity and even pride keep people from accessing their victory. Look at Psalms 139:14, *"I praise thee; for I am fearfully and wonderfully made: marvellous are Thy works; and that my soul knoweth right well."* Right now I want you to get up and go find a mirror and look directly into it and say this OUT LOUD, "I am the most marvelous thing that God has ever created. I was carefully, fearfully, and wonderfully made in the same image of God. What I see in this mirror, and what others see when they look at me is EXACTLY what He wanted me to be. For this, I PRAISE YOU LORD!"

Racism is a vile stronghold that comes against the creative authority of God or God's creation—YOU. How does it accomplish this? As I mentioned before, racism is the mindset that YOU (God's creation) are not fit. Racism says, "YOU can't do it." Racism seeks to disqualify you from fulfilling your purpose. Racism discourages, demoralizes, and deters you from pursuing the destiny of God. Racism tells you that you are unfit because of your heritage, unfit because of your skin color, or your nationality. It says you are unable because of your educational background, your economic status, or your physical attributes. Bound in the heart of man, racism points out every difference and highlights every shortcoming. Racism sets others up as more able than you; superior, greater, more qualified, and better equipped.

My brethren, have not the faith of our Lord Jesus Christ, the Lord of glory, with respect of persons.

For if there come unto your assembly a man with a gold ring, in goodly apparel, and there come in also a poor man in vile raiment;

And ye have respect to him that weareth the gay clothing, and say unto him, Sit thou here in a good place; and say to the poor, Stand thou there, or sit here under my footstool:

*Are ye not then partial in yourselves,
and are become judges of evil thoughts?*

*Hearken, my beloved brethren, Hath not
God chosen the poor of this world rich in
faith, and heirs of the kingdom which he
hath promised to them that love him?*

*But ye have despised the poor. Do
not rich men oppress you, and draw
you before the judgment seats?*

*Do not they blaspheme that worthy name
by the which ye are called?*

*If ye fulfill the royal law according
to the scripture, Thou shalt love thy
neighbour as thyself, ye do well:*

*But if ye have respect to persons,
ye commit sin, and are convinced
of the law as transgressors.*

*For whosoever shall keep the whole law, and
yet offend in one point, he is guilty of all.*

James 2:1-10 KJV

Racism is a respector of persons. Racism negates
the influence and authority of God by substituting

Only when you see yourself and others through the eyes of Christ are you truly liberated from the bondages of racism.

its own ideas of worth above the calling and anointing of God. Before you can crack the Apostolic and Prophetic Code and transform your realm of influence, you must first tear down the stronghold of racism. You must be free from its grip and fully confident of who you are in Christ. You must also be free from its grip by allowing others to be who they are in Christ, and not limited by your judgments of their worth. Only when you see yourself and others through the eyes of Christ are you truly liberated from the bondages of racism.

The Price of Apostolic and Prophetic Life

If you are an apostle or prophet, or if you embrace the apostolic or prophetic, then one of the fruits of your life, ministry, business, and church are that it will not only attract, but that it will embrace different nationalities and races on all levels. You are not one of God's holy apostles and prophets unless you have and are in covenant relationships with people of different races, nationalities, abilities, and gender! That is right. I don't care what title you carry, if you are unable to submit to authority because it comes in the form of a woman, or from one who is younger than you, or of a different color than you, then YOU ARE A RACIST!

The first woman that a man submits to, is his mother. She is an authority figure in his life from the day of his birth. After he leaves his mother (and father), the Bible says that he cleaves to his wife. Now every husband must submit to his wife! It took me years to get this revelation—and it cost me $100,000's. All because I didn't (and wouldn't) listen to the counsel of my wife. Your wife may not fully understand your business, or know everything about your ministry, but God put something in her when he created her for you. He took her out of your side so she would be able to KNOW and be able to SEE THINGS about you and for you THAT NO ONE ELSE CAN SEE! She can see what an intercessor can't see, what a prophet can't see, what a business partner can't see. Why? "Because she is all of that and a bag a chips!" God says that when a man finds a wife he finds a good thing and obtains favor from God (Proverbs 18:22).

I submit that every one of us is a racist on *some* level (perhaps even sub-consciously) and needs to be delivered! I'm not suggesting that we are born that way, and I'm certainly not saying that it is the devil's fault. In fact, the next time you are near a play ground or day care center or church nursery, look at the toddlers. You will see children of all ages, races, sizes, and gender happily playing, hugging, sharing, and laughing together with no problem. Then, take a look at their parents, they will be hanging around in groups, divided according to their racial, religious, political or economic beliefs—that is, unless they have been delivered!

Choices

When my wife and I attend an event, business meeting, church function, or whatever—anywhere that there will be people, we ALWAYS make sure not to fall into the trap of speaking to black people first or even to Christians first. We make a conscious decision to seek out those who are different from us and initiate conversations with them.

I will never forget my mother's reaction the first time that I brought a white girlfriend home. My mom was so super nice to her, but when she left to go to the rest room my mother asked me, "What is *she* doing here?" I asked her, "Who?" She said, "You know who." I couldn't help myself. I answered, "No, who?" I made her say it, I made her look at me and say "THE WHITE GIRL."

I still remember telling her, "I thought you told me that we weren't prejudiced. I thought you told me that color didn't matter." My mom looked at me, totally embarrassed and shocked at how she had just acted. She apologized, and it was sincere. This young girl was from a very wealthy family. I was from an upper middle class family and lived right across from the country club, but none of that mattered. Her family did not want us to date because I was black. So, her parents sent her off to Maryland to live until she got over our relationship. I won't share details, but the family broke apart and the young girl's life took a sad and sinful turn. Now, I am not saying that her parent's decision to keep us from seeing each other was the source of their problems. What I am saying is that their decision to send her away was rooted in racism, and I know that decision had negative and long-lasting consequences for their entire family.

God Has a Sense of Humor

I got saved and delivered in a church that was 99.9% white—AND it was also COUNTRY-WESTERN! Oh boy, does God have a sense of humor when He wants to deliver you. I was a young black man, fresh out of prison. My culture and my music had taught me that the white man was my enemy! So, God sent me to an almost all white church that was country-western and had very few young people there except for my wife and me. God used that pastor in my life, and he married us. He was my spiritual father for eight years, put trust and confidence back into me, and opened the door for deliverance from the spirit of racism. I will never forget the day my pastor gave me the keys to the church. I remember telling him that I could not accept them. He asked me why and I told him that I was no good and a criminal. I will never forget what he said, "You are not that person anymore son. You are a born again child of God and I trust you. God sent you here to help me build and pastor this church." Praise God for true *four-walled* pastors that have a heart for the people of God. Ten years later my criminal record was sealed, giving me a clean profile!

I remember several years ago when Dr. Fred Price of Crenshaw Christian Center started preaching a series on national television entitled "Race, Religion and Racism." The church, the media, and the Christian community went crazy. They could not handle it. They even asked him if he had to preach it that way! There is no "polite" or "politically correct" way to deal with racism. You must EXPOSE IT, and then CAST IT OUT! Cast it out of your mind, your mouth, your heart, your ministry, your home, and your business!

You and I have heard for years that the most segregated day of the week is Sunday morning. Let's rise up together through the three gates of heaven (the church, the marketplace, and the workplace) and change the world!

Let me ask you a quick, but personal question? If your son or daughter came home with a girlfriend, boyfriend, fiancé or even a new spouse of a different race, culture, or nationality how would you react? Let's go deeper. What would you do when they had children? Would you love those grandchildren without prejudice?

> NOTE: If this area is still a struggle for you please write or email me so that I can pray for you. I give you my word that this information and your situation will be held in the strictest confidence, and will not be shared with anyone. My desire is to help you walk in God's total freedom and deliverance for your life.

Before we move on to the next chapter, I want to leave you with a smile on your face. Do you realize that when God destroyed the earth by flood, the only ones that made it into the ark were members of the animal kingdom and Noah, his sons, and their wives? What I find most interesting is that there was a total of only eight people that were saved from the flood and on that ark. So, if you really want to be technical and know the truth, every human being in the world—no matter what color, culture, or country—had to come from those eight that were originally on that ark. Remember, God made us from the dust of the earth and in the end, our physical bodies will be returned back into the earth where they came from.

SUMMARY POINTS

○ Before you can crack the Apostolic and Prophetic Code, you must also understand that there are three gates of hell.

○ Each of these gates represents a blockade to the fulfillment of your destiny. They are: religion, tradition, and racism.

○ Each of these gates is really a stronghold, a mindset that keeps people in bondage, operating from a flawed perspective, and unable to experience the fullness of God's Kingdom purpose.

Gate One: Religion

Religion places the focus on man and away from God. It is filled with rules, regulations, and a hierarchy of power. It diminishes relationship with God, challenges and stresses relationship with family and friends, and seeks to control.

Gate Two: Tradition

Tradition sets itself above the authority of God's Word. Locked into a pattern or routine, it keeps people blind and bound. The fetters (chains) of tradition hinder people from expanding their boundaries and being released to exercise dominion.

Gate Three: Racism

Racism seeks to disqualify others. Racism is evil and thwarts the purposes of God in favor of its own superiority and power. The only cure for racism is deliverance.

RAISED UP AND RELEASED

ℰꙨ Cℛ

The early church scattered due to persecution. The church is being scattered today due to rejection! My wife, Darlene, and I were faithful leaders and faithful members in the *four-walled* church for 19 years before God released us out and into our own ministry. During those 19 years we were members of three churches. The first church we served for eight years, the second one for seven years, and the third one for four years. But during all those years I, my ministry, and my dreams were always rejected by the leaders of the *four-walled* church. When I would try and share them with the senior pastor, deacons, and elders I was rejected, but when I went outside the four walls of the church, I was fully accepted and embraced. My wife experienced even greater rejection, because she didn't have to work outside the home, always drove a nice car, dressed nice, and was always excited about the things of God. I can't tell you how many times she was passed over, over-looked, and under appreciated. We have always been great givers, great servants, and loved the people of God, BUT we never fully felt accepted by our own *four-walled* church leaders. Leaders that we worked along side of during those 19 years.

One thing that my wife, my children, and I had to get delivered from once we stepped out into our own ministry was the spirit of rejection! Thank God for deliverance. Apostle John Eckhardt, who is our primary spiritual covering, was the first minister, man of God, and apostle that fully accepted me, my ministry, and my mantle. This caused me to shift to a HIGHER place in God and in the Kingdom. My wife and I had been ordained twice previously, but when this apostle and prophetic company ordained us and laid their hands on us, ALL REJECTION left and the ability to ADVANCE as his spiritual son and daughter entered into our hearts, spirit, and mantle! Now we have that same ability to go out and activate others into their ministry, gifts, and calling.

I remember one statement that Apostle John Eckhardt said during our ordination. He said, "everything that I have, I impart it into you, and all of the necessary grace that you need now and in the days to come, and you will go out and impart it into others." If you are a *four-walled* church leader or pastor, please impart and release everything that you have to the next generation. This is what you are meant to do!

Recently, I received a phone call from Apostle John P. Kelly asking me, "How are doing, son? How is your business going?" He wanted to know what was going on in my ministry, and he wanted to let me know that he was praying for me and my family. He wanted me to understand that he was in my corner, and that as my family and I succeeded, and that as we achieved greater levels of success, that is what would make him successful. I can't tell you the feelings of security, affirmation, and confidence that this gives a human being. It is marvelous to be in covenant with real apostles, and to have true apostolic covering and connection!

Do you know why my wife and I have the best spiritual covering and connections on the earth? It is because we are the best that God has and for over twenty years we served the best, gave the best, and when our time came, He gave us the best—Apostle John Eckhardt and Apostle John P. Kelly. He gave them to us so that we could go out and raise up and release the best "YOU" into your Kingdom assignment, place, and authority! Again, if you are a *four-walled* church leader or pastor, please recognize those that God has placed in your midst, bless them, honor them, raise them up publicly, and release them. It's the greatest ministry that you have. And guess what? When you do this, those that are called to you will stay and even those that aren't called to stay with you, will still go out from you with blessings and change the world—all because you were obedient to raise up and release!

Wouldn't it be strange for our children at age 20, 25, 35, or 45 years old to still be living at home? When we moved our youngest son off to college in 2007 it was two days before his 18th birthday. I prophesied boldly over all three of my sons, declaring that they would be out by their 18th birthday. Let me tell you what happened to me as we were getting ready to head back home. Several days earlier we had prayed for him and as we were getting ready to drive away, suddenly I became overwhelmed by emotions that I had never experienced before. I began to weep uncontrollably because the moment, the day, and the hour had come that I had to release him to fulfill his destiny. At that moment, I wasn't sure not only if he was ready, but I wasn't sure if I was ready. Did I do enough? Did I put enough in him to launch him to succeed? I will never forget what he said as we stood there embracing one another. He said, "Dad, I am going to make you proud and you will see that you were a great father. I am going to stay focused and do what God put me on the earth to do." As I am writing this,

I am crying remembering that moment. Next week he is coming home for his first summer break and I can't tell you how proud his mom and I are of him. Pastors, when you see and hear about the success of those that you released and helped along the way, it WILL CHANGE YOUR LIFE FOREVER!

Today a great tragedy has occurred. Many apostles, prophets, pastors, or *four-walled* church leaders have failed to raise up and have not released ANY of their sons and daughters. They are not preparing the next generation of leaders that will guarantee the success of the church or of the Kingdom of God! In Jeremiah 10:20-21 AMP it says, *"My tabernacle is spoiled, and all my cords (connections) are broken: my children are gone forth of me, and they are not: there is none to stretch forth my tent any more, and to set up my curtains (coverings). For the pastors are become brutish (grossly ruthless or unfeeling as, enslaving the people), and have not sought the LORD: therefore they shall not prosper, and all their flocks shall be scattered."* Leaders have failed to raise up Kingdom Representatives or kings in the marketplace.

Church leaders have failed to raise up Kingdom Representatives in the marketplace.

Instead, they build ever-widening hierarchies that inflate their influence and broaden the reach of their ministry, but yield less and less impact on society.

There is an attempt by church leaders to label everyone inside a *four-walled* church—making them a deacon, an elder, an usher, a greeter, associate pastor, etc. And yet, not all are called to function in the *four-walled* church. Why is there such an attempt to keep all talents, gifts and callings at work only inside the *four-walled* establishment when God has clearly called us to GO into the world (KOSMOS) and preach the gospel of the Kingdom of Heaven which is at hand? God desires for us to duplicate a successful Kingdom pattern of global dominance. Instead, the church tightens its hold on productive men and women, calling on them for greater commitment, greater participation, more meetings, a busier schedule, more giving, more, more, more... The end result is that the quality of life goes down for those who are most heavily committed to the establishment (the *four-walled* church). Their families suffer, their marriages suffer, their performance on the job, or their attention to their businesses all suffer in the name of building the Kingdom when in fact we're just having church or a religious activity.

Instead of being better at what they do, bringing honor to the Name of Jesus and demonstrating the power and authority of Christ at work within, they lag behind others in the world system who focus in their field and excel. This spiral can only end in frustration. Eventually, the person will either backslide to escape the mounting pressures of church life, or their personal life will languish. These people are caught in a terrible cycle of religion and tradition and learn to cope by putting on a plastic shell that tells others they are holy—even when their life is empty and void of purpose.

As a Wealth Strategist that helps Americans and Baby Boomers retire younger, richer, and wealthier, I find it very interesting that when tithing, long-term, committed Christians or church members come into my office for a financial review, there are normally two areas in their lives that are really out of whack. Number one—their family, and number two—their finances. They really aren't spending quality time with their own children or spouses. Many of them are estranged from their immediate family, and for no apparent reason. They're barely getting by financially and in most cases, are living month to month, have very little savings, and hardly any retirement funds. They rarely take vacations and have no emergency fund, but yet every week they are tithing, giving offerings, and hearing the Word preached to them. They are having no RADICAL changes or breakthroughs occurring. SOMETHING IS WRONG WITH THIS PICTURE!

I have to advise them to continue their tithe, but to refrain from giving extra until they can get a handle on their finances. My next instruction is for them to take some of their money and spend it on their family, their children, or even on themselves. Now I am not encouraging people to go into debt, but I AM encouraging them to start enjoying life. If they don't, they will end up with *no* life—bankrupt or divorced! I believe that any *four-walled* church leader, pastor, or ministry that continues to receive tithes, offerings, or ANY financial seeds from a member, and doesn't know what is going on in the life of that individual, doesn't really understand covering and will be judged by God for it. When a person tithes to you, it places a demand on your anointing and covering. How can you cover what you don't know or understand?

You need to enjoy life!

In the last chapter, I told you that my wife and I go out dancing, to comedy clubs, and to jazz concerts. When we go dancing, I am not trying to be a prophet, a "public" Christian, or the man of God! I am operating within the creative ability that God Himself put inside of me as a man when he created me to romance, satisfy, and stimulate my wife to a place of excitement, attraction, and joy that she has never known before. And we are not listening to "Hosanna" or "Meet me at the Cross" at the time. And now, after

20 years of marriage, and 25 years of being together, we are more attracted to each other today then we were when we first met. We still spend about 90% of our time together, and when I travel for ministry and business we travel as a team!

Your Greatest Wealth

Your greatest wealth comes in three forms. They are: number one—your family or closest friends. Number two—your time, and number three—your money! The main purpose for the apostolic and the prophetic, and for the ministry of apostles, prophets, and the five-fold ministry office gifts is to PERFECT THE SAINTS FOR THE WORK OF THE MINISTRY (Ephesians 4:8-16). Your first and most important ministry before the *four-walled* church, and before your business or career, is your family. You and I only get one chance in this life to raise our children right—one chance with our spouse to develop a happy, love-filled marriage. I believe that if you have a happy home and a happy marriage you will AUTOMATICALLY have a GREATER CHURCH with STRONGER, more STABLE, and more PRODUCTIVE saints. God is not going to do away with the *four-walled* church, He established it. I am not even trying to imply that, but how we have had church and where we have gathered is going to change!

In Jeremiah 23:1-4 God says, *"He will set up shepherds over the flock which shall feed them (with rev-*

elation)." Luke 11:49 says, *"I will send you prophets and apostles and them will you slay and persecute."*

The sign of a REAL apostle or apostolic leader is the sons and daughters that they have raised up and released—not just in their church, but beyond the church, functioning OUTSIDE of their ministry and now functioning on their OWN in MINISTRY, raising up and releasing others into THEIR OWN ministry! This is the main purpose of the apostolic and the prophetic.

A Better Plan

How much better would it be if the *four-walled* church leaders would call people out (publicly) and raise them up and release them to take dominion? What level of success is possible if the *four-walled* church leaders recognized those with a marketplace or workplace calling and publicly confirmed them, ordained them, and laid hands on them, releasing them out of the *four-walled* church to be five-fold ministers in the marketplace? These marketplace leaders should be recognized as having the same level of authority as ministers that went through seminary. They should merit the same level of respect as those behind the pulpit. They should be recognized as those who have authority just like Jesus did (Matthew 10). What influence would be felt in society if these people were set in their rightful place in the church, in the marketplace, and in the workplace? How far and how fast would the Kingdom of God advance in the earth if

God's people were established to rule and reign in the sphere of authority that God has called them to?

What would happen if the Body of Christ would crack the Apostolic and Prophetic Code, learn to operate within their function, and raise people up in the *four-walled* church, in the marketplace, and in the workplace? When this happens—and it's already started—a revolution will take place. This will be Kingdom and global dominance of all of the world's systems in the marketplace.

Bishop Bill Hamon calls it *The Day of the Saints* or the *Third and Final Apostolic Reformation*. Bishop Hamon goes on to state, "that in the Saints Movement (which began in 2007), the average saint will have a ministry greater than Billy Graham, Benny Hinn, Oral Roberts, and T.L. Osborn!" When God's people are equipped with understanding and released to walk within their authority, exercise dominion, and advance the Kingdom of God, a revival or a prophetic awakening such as has never been seen before will take place. This will be even greater than what took place in the book of Acts with the early church and apostles! Then and only then, will the significant transfer of wealth begin to flow into the Kingdom of God, and into the hands of Kingdom Representatives that have been selected by God, released, and raised up by apostles and prophets who will know how, where, and with whom to distribute this wealth.

Give it Away!

Apostle John P. Kelly says, "The true purpose of wealth is to give it away." This wealth creation and wealth distribution will flood the Body of Christ with resources, influence, and fame—allowing every area of society to be transformed and penetrated with the government of God. I believe that any *four-walled* church that does not embrace the apostolic and the prophetic, and does not raise up and release sons and daughters and five-fold ministers out into the marketplace will not be allowed access to the transfer of wealth.

The greatest transfer of wealth is the harvest of souls! Only real apostolic and prophetic fathers will have access to these souls, which will then give us access into their territories, which will in turn give us access into their industries or realms. This will allow us to begin ruling and reigning in the ENTIRE world! Now THAT is global dominance. Only then will the stage be set for Jesus Christ to actually come back! The transfer of wealth goes far beyond tithes and offerings. The transfer of wealth is not for

The greatest transfer of wealth is the harvest of souls!

the purposes of paying a pastor a bigger salary. It is not for the purpose of building a bigger and better church facility. It is not for the purpose of just funding in-house church programs. It is not just for the purpose of Kingdom Representatives having a greater net worth, buying more cars, houses, etc. The purpose of the transfer of wealth is so that we can rule and reign and exercise dominion in the earth.

> *The purpose of the transfer of wealth is so that we can rule and reign and exercise dominion in the earth.*

How do you take over a city? By buying it! Owning real estate, owning businesses, etc. There are many programs in your city and territory (that may or may not be Christian based) that need funding to function and thrive. Programs that help children, seniors, and single mothers, that improve education, etc., and the list go on and on. This is where the wealth needs to be distributed! Why? Because it is your city, territory, or region and this is how you will make it better—by changing it through the influence and wealth that God has placed into your hands?

The purpose of wealth is also for transforming nations. It is to finance sending teams to the nations so that the world can be changed! There are apostles and prophets, and apostolic and prophetic teams that we must fund and finance. For some of us, generating wealth to finance ministry is a large part of our calling. For some of us, we need to be traveling with these teams, because that is also a part of our ministry. We are not just called to finance these projects, but also to go to nations, because you may have a word and an anointing to change economies, countries, tribes, and nations! There are roughly six billion people on planet earth. There is enough wealth that if it was equally divided among all six billion people—each person would end up with about $2 million dollars. Sounds good doesn't it? The only problem is that within a few years all of the wealth will end up back into the hands of the 20% that have it now, because they are the ones that produced it. God is real funny about who He allows access to real Kingdom and biblical wealth.

In the next chapter, I will begin to unfold the elements of the Apostolic and Prophetic Code. You will see why it is vital to understand your calling, to be authorized in your assignment or assigned place, and to take dominion. You were called to influence and transform your territory, region, city, and industry. Only when you understand the mysteries by revelation can you walk out into the kingdoms and realms, knowing your assignment, ready to succeed and TAKE OVER!

To take over means: to assume control, management, or responsibility for; to become dominant; or to deal a blow to, strike or hit

Jesus said, *"Greater works will YOU DO"* (John 14:12). How will they or can they be greater? Because it will be YOU doing it and not HIM. We expected Jesus to do it, but guess what? He expects YOU to do it in this day, in this hour—in our lifetime, and in our generation!

THE APOSTOLIC PARADIGM

ℰꙨ ℭℜ

There is an office gift of apostle found in Ephesians 4:11 and in 1 Corinthians 12:28, but every Christian is not called to be an apostle. Every Christian can, however, become apostolic. I highly recommend you to read *Leadershift* or, *A Shift In Leaders* by Apostle John Eckhardt. In this book, Apostle Eckhardt moves your thinking from the pastoral into the apostolic and prophetic. This paradigm adjustment is necessary in order to fully embrace what God is doing in the earth today.

Before we move on, let me define two words—*paradigm* and *apostolic*. Webster's Dictionary defines the word paradigm as: an example, pattern, model or way of thinking; especially an outstandingly clear or typical example; or, a framework.

According to Stephen Covey's *Seven Habits of highly Effective People*, "paradigms are generally defined as the way we see the world, not through visual sight but through our perceptions, understanding, and interpreting *(page 23)*." They are like maps and "each of us has many, many maps in our head, which can be divided into two main categories: maps of the way things are, (or realities) and maps of the way things should be, (or values). We interpret everything we experience through these mental maps *(page 24)*."

Keeping this concept of paradigms in mind, consider that the church of today *is* operating inside a distinctly pastoral paradigm. It is necessary that the church move out of this paradigm and into an apostolic one. Apostle John Eckhardt explains that the word "apostolic" is an adjective that describes the characteristic of an apostle. All can be (or become) apostolic, although not all *are* apostles. Apostolic describes the traits and dimensions of a "sent one" who is "first in order" or "first of its kind." An apostolic anointing is a *sending*

An apostolic paradigm revolves around the concept of sending and being sent.

anointing and a *governing* anointing. Furthermore, we can not be genuinely "apostolic" if we reject the ministry of the apostle. **So, an apostolic paradigm revolves around the concept of sending and being sent.**

The call to be an apostle or prophet comes directly from God Himself. It comes before any man, woman, or organization ever recognizes or acknowledges it. An apostle or prophet is not ruled over by an organization, denomination, or a man. God is their covering. Then, as God covers them, they connect in relationships to other apostles and prophets for greater authority and mutual accountability. A true apostle or prophet serves as a pastor, shepherd, or leader to God's five-fold ministers and Kingdom Representatives. They are called and set over territories and nations.

God never called pastors to pastor churches—He called them to pastor people! Pastors don't release sheep—they herd them—it's their nature. This may be tough to swallow, but there is no scriptural evidence for the title, "Senior Pastor." And even though people ascribe to become a pastor and view this as the highest "public" or "pulpit" ministry, there is in fact a higher "rank" than pastor—apostles and prophets.

Apostles and prophets can be called to pastor churches, and they are certainly called to have apostolic oversight of leaders and networks (of churches). Government is their nature. Their mantle and authority is to raise up, release, and send out. They have a governmental anointing, where a pastor has more of a managerial anointing. For this reason, many *four-walled* pastors need to make a paradigm shift. This will not eliminate pastoral ministry, but rather enhance it. This shift will result in positive changes in the way ministry is conducted. Greater things will occur—signs, wonders, revelation, power, wisdom, and a greater release of the saints will result. *(Source: Apostle John Eckhardt)*

An apostle is a "sent one." An apostle establishes the order of God and can be related to in terms similar to a commander-in-chief, a general, or even an ambassador. The first gift, office, and authority that God set in the church was apostle (1 Corinthians 12:28). This, along with the gift (office and authority) of the prophet are the foundation of the Church of Jesus Christ, or the New Testament Church (Ephesians 2:20). But at the core, an apostolic paradigm revolves around the concept of sending and being sent with a *specific purpose* and normally to a *specific group of people* and to a *specific region and territory.* In marketing this is identified as a target market—in the Body of Christ, we call it an assignment!

If you don't know where you are called to go, how will you know when you get there? If not, anywhere you happen to wind up will do. If you don't know who you are called to, then there is a possibility that you may be talking to the wrong group of people! God is an apostolic God, and He is very specific. He told Noah when, where, and how to build the ark? He also told him what to put inside of it, and Noah's obedience saved his entire family.

God told Jonah what city to cry against (Jonah 1:2). He didn't send the angel Gabriel to three or four virgins, He was sent specifically to Mary and overshadowed her only (Luke 1:26-38). Prophecy is the same way—it is specific and not general when released by a mature prophet or prophetic person. We must embrace the idea that we are sent by God, anointed and appointed to carry out our purpose, authorized to establish God's order, and be His representatives in the Kingdom. You were, are, and always will be God's first choice. He was very specific when He created you, why He created you, and even about who your parents were. Why? Because He needed their DNA to complete you. Your parents were needed for your conception, but they may not be necessary for you to fulfill your destiny! So, if you were born out of wedlock, from hardship, rape, or incest—it DOESN'T MATTER! Maybe you never met your parents, or were abandoned at birth, or adopted. It DOESN'T MATTER! You are here now on earth and God expects you to make a difference in the world, because He is the One Who created you.

God didn't intend for you to be born through hardship or sin, but He did intend for you to get here. Now it is up to you to do something that makes a difference in the world! You have no excuse not to succeed. This is a necessary paradigm for us to embrace. Apostles and apostolic people are pioneers and they should always be blazing new trails or traveling a course where we have never been before.

Positioned for Destiny

Shifting causes you to get in the right place at the right time, so that you can GO in the right (new) direction! Mark 16:15 says, *"GO (YOU) INTO all the world..."*

The Greek word for go is POREUOMAI. It means to travel, depart, go away from, go forth, make or take a journey, or walk. God told Abraham to get out of his country (land), and away from his family and from his father's house and go to a (new) land that He would show Him (Genesis 12:1). God didn't describe the land to Abraham. He didn't reveal any of its qualities or describe the landscape, but He expected that Abraham would know in his spirit that it was the right land once he got there. Now THAT is apostolic revelation!

The Greek word for world is KOSMOS. It means the sum total of the material universe, the beauty in it, and the total of the persons living in the world. Land is the physical evidence of heaven! What are your boundaries? Where are you permitted to go? Where are you not permitted to go? It is important for us to understand our boundaries because we don't have authority to be everywhere. This is one reason why I believe that you have to be very careful when you relocate—especially if your company sends you. You better make darn sure that is what God has for you and you aren't relocating just for more money or for a change of life. When you get to the new place, you will still be *you*. If you were financially challenged *before* you left, and if you didn't really like your life *before* you left, relocation alone will not make these situations improve. In fact, if you have moved for your own reasons and they are not in line with God's purpose and destiny for you, then you are headed for trouble! Now, you still have the same problems you had before, but they are compounded because you are completely out of order and removed from the boundaries where you were granted authority and protection.

The devil may have power (though limited), but we have authority! God told us, *"Ask of Me, and I will give you the nations (people and territories) as your inheritance, and the uttermost parts of the earth as your possession"* (Psalm 2:8 AMP). We are called to rule and reign (Revelation 5:10). We have been raised up together, and made to sit together in heavenly places in Christ Jesus (Ephesians 2:6).

Two Types of Shifting

There are two types of shifting that must take place in order for us to be permitted into new areas or boundaries. They are:

○ One: A shift in leaders must take place. *Leader-Shift* is a book about moving from the pastoral into the apostolic and the prophetic. This book is a must read if you are ready to move forward. We must fully embrace, without any doubt or reservations, the apostolic and the prophetic. This CAN NOT be done unless you believe in apostles and prophets, and are in relationship with them.

○ Two: A shift in mantles must take place. *Man-tleShift* is my next book. In it, I will talk about moving from man's "FOOL TIME" ministry and moving into His (Jesus') "FULL TIME" ministry! If you are in the marketplace or in the work place, then you are *already* in FULL TIME ministry! Study the life of Jesus and the apostles once Jesus came out of the wilderness. He said, "Repent and follow Me, for the Kingdom of Heaven is at hand." They were IMMEDIATELY in FULL TIME ministry and stayed busy OUTSIDE the *four-walled* church—functioning in their gate or assigned place, and *then* went into the synagogue teaching and trying to show them a better way!

Shifting causes you to get in the right place so that you can GO in the right direction.

Two Types of Change

There are also two types of change that must occur in order for us to be permitted into new areas or boundaries.

○ One: Our thought patterns and mental processes must occur. Our thinking must change and come up to a much higher level. This is why prophetic teaching is so important and must go beyond just preaching.

○ Two: A change in our language or terminology must occur. On the day of Pentecost something very unusual happened. They received a God-like ability to INSTANTLY be able to speak every known language that man spoke at that time. Amazingly, they did this without any training, schooling, experience, coaching, or teaching (Acts 2:1-8). Why were they able to do this? Because it was the right time and they were positioned in the right place to do the right assignment—to take dominion over their known world! Guess what? YOU AND I have that same right. We cannot take over the world's systems without realizing what occurs when we are filled with the Holy Ghost. The first thing we receive is power, and one of the first evidences of this is that we receive a God-like ability **to speak every man's language** in the marketplace (See Acts 2:1-8)!

Throughout history, restoration always causes reformation.

Throughout history, restoration always causes reformation (a change that makes things better) which releases new thought patterns. Every new release or new revelation also brings a new language with it. Look at Starbucks. They created their own names for things that weren't even in the dictionary! Now, we walk up in their lines ordering drinks with names that no other store offers. Even if you just want a small drink, *you have to use their terminology to be understood.* To get a small drink at Starbucks, you have to ask for a tall? e-Bay created their own name and developed a new system. The Internet is a whole different world—filled with a new language that you accept and learn to use, or get left behind. You must adapt to words like blog, codes, crawlers, gateways, flash, html, streaming video, e-commerce and on and on!

Every new revelation brings a new covenant! When God released us out of the *four-walled* church, I was wondering why no one was calling us, or desiring to fellowship with us. And then I heard Apostle Pat Francis say "when God gives you a new revelation or births something new in you, you become an orphan. And then He will put you in covenant with someone new." Never forget that you and I are only one key relationship—one new covenant away from success!

Expanding Territory and Dominion

"Enlarge your house; build an addition; spread out your home! For you will soon be bursting at the seams. Your descendants will take over other nations and live in their cities.

Isaiah 54:2-3 NLT

For I will cast out the nations before you and enlarge your borders;

Exodus 34:24 NKJV

Jesus took the church into the world, and the world came to church. How do we know this?

- ○ The woman with the issue of blood *came to Him* (Mark 5:24-34)

- ○ The centurion ruler *came to Him* because his servant was sick (Matthew 8:5-13)

- ○ Jarius, a ruler of the synagogue, *approached Him* about his sick daughter (Mark 5:21-35)

- ○ The crazy, demon possessed man on the island *approached Him* (Mark 5:1-15)

- ○ Blind Bartimaeus, when he had heard that it was Jesus of Nazareth passing by, *cried out to Him* (Mark 10:46-52)

○ For those who *came to Him*: the blind received sight, the lepers were cleansed, the deaf heard, the dead were raised, the poor had the gospel preached to them (Matthew 11:5)

There is no Scripture reference found where Jesus sets up a tent or pavilion or rally and waits for people to come receive Him. Instead, we find that He was approached while He was on His way somewhere, or was when He was already at a location and in the process of ministering to someone else. The point is this—*they all came to Him*. Jesus did not go out of His way to get to them; they went out of their way to get to Him! The *four-walled* church system was already set up in Jesus' day just like it is today. And yet, Jesus didn't schedule healing meetings, revival services, or new members classes. Jesus did not come to do away with these things, but He DID come to take the Kingdom of God *into* the WORLD—into the world's systems, into the world's societies, and most certainly into the world's marketplace!

What we've have been trying to do for the last 2000 years, is get the world to come to church. And then, after we think of any way we can to get them in the door, we try as hard as we can to make them "churchy." As a result, the church has become worldly—and believe me, the world is a whole lot better at being worldly. So, in essence, we have become a poor counterfeit and to the world, we appear as valuable as cheap, dime store knock-offs. Why should they be impressed? Look at this Scripture:

But God has chosen the foolish things of the world to put to shame the wise, and God has chosen the weak things of the world to put to shame the things which are mighty; and the base things of the world and the things which are despised God has chosen, and the things which are not, to bring to nothing the things that are, that no flesh should glory in His presence.

I Corinthians 1:27-30 NKJV

At the Tower of Babel, when the world tried to get to heaven by their own endeavors, God sent a spirit of confusion and changed their language (Genesis 11:1-9).

When God wanted heaven to get to the earth, He sent the spirit of agreement and gave every one in the upper room the ability, authority, and power to speak in tongues—so that every man could hear the message in his own language. In this case, God "un-confused" things, giving man supernatural ability to communicate (Acts 2:1-13).

Greater Revelation

Never forget that apostles (and therefore the apostolic) carry a greater level of revelation. In 1998,

Marilyn Hickey walked out onto the platform at the church where my wife and I were leaders, and made this statement, "You can always tell when you are in the presence of a real apostle, because of the level of revelation that is being released in the room or atmosphere." That so blessed me, because it didn't matter what subject our apostle was preaching on back then, when I left the service I always had *new revelation* for my business, life, and ministry. Whenever my wife and I are in Chicago attending Apostle Eckhardt's Crusaders Church, the moment that I walk into that building, the revelation and clarity of the voice of God is almost overwhelming.

Webster's Dictionary defines revelation as: an act of revealing or communicating divine truth; something that is revealed by God to humans; an act of revealing to view or making known; something that is revealed, especially an enlightening or astonishing disclosure (shocking revelations): a pleasant often enlightening surprise.

In *The Dictionary of the Apostolic* (page 266) Apostle John Eckhardt defines revelation for us. Revelation comes from the Greek word APOKALUPSIS meaning disclosure, manifestation, revelation (Ephesians 3:3). Apostolic ministry is a ministry of revelation. Revelation is the foundation of apostolic authority (Matthew 16:17-19). **Those who have revelation have the keys of the Kingdom.** Apostles understand and preach the mysteries of God through revelation. There are certain revelations the church will not have without apostles and prophets.

Revelation is revealed knowledge or "know how" for the purpose of knowing mysteries. All truth has not been revealed, but all truth is revealed in Scripture, and this is the main purpose of the apostolic and the prophetic—to release a present, current, fresh, and relevant truth for today. Every apostle and prophet can have a piece of, or a particular truth that has to be released in their generation (See John 14:6, John 16:13, 1 John 4:6). Now, let's look at the following:

So then, let us (apostles) be looked upon as ministering servants of Christ and stewards (trustees) of the mysteries (the secret purposes) of God.

1 Corinthians 4:1 AMP

The word stewards comes from the Greek word, OIKONOMOS and means to administer. A steward is a person who manages the domestic affairs of a family. A steward is also a treasurer, and the term applies to apostles and ministers of the gospel, but also to private believers (1 Peter 4:10).

As each of you has received a gift (a particular spiritual talent, a gracious divine endowment), employ it for one another as (befits) good trustees of God's many-sided grace (faithful stewards of the extremely Diverse powers and gifts granted to Christians by unmerited favor).

1 Peter 4:10 AMP

The word mysteries comes from the Greek word MUSTERION and means to close or shut. A mystery is some secret, hidden thing, or a secret which is naturally unknown to human reason and is only known by the revelation of God that has never been seen before. In other generations, such a thing was not made known to the sons of man as it is now revealed to His holy apostles and prophets by the Spirit. This is not extra-biblical revelation, but instead it is revelation that comes from the Word of God. It isn't "spooky," it is revelation that can be validated from Scripture for the benefit of the Kingdom of God and not for any man's glory.

(This mystery) was never disclosed to human beings in past generations as it has now been revealed to His holy apostles (consecrated messengers) and prophets by the (Holy) Spirit.

Ephesians 3:5 AMP

Now that we have discussed the Apostolic Paradigm, we will move on to discover the Prophetic Paradigm.

ℰℴ ℭℬ

CHAPTER FIVE

THE PROPHETIC PARADIGM

ℰℴ ℭℬ

As with the gift of apostle, there is also an office gift of prophet (Ephesians 4:11). Again, not every Christian is called to be a prophet, but every Christian is permitted to prophesy (1 Corinthians 14:31) and should be prophetic. Both the Old and New Testaments are filled with God's prophets, declaring the Word of the Lord, revealing God's plan, and activating His purpose.

Surely the Sovereign LORD does nothing without revealing his plan to his servants the prophets.

Amos 3:7 NIV

Denying the power and relevance of the prophetic in your life, business, ministry, and church is like denying oxygen to your lungs. Prophetic words initiate, exhort, comfort, shift, establish, change, set in order, release, identify, clarify, launch, and confirm. Prophetic utterances activate and release the plans and purposes of God. Prophetic words declare and unfold. **Prophetic words are creative and have supernatural weight and authority.**

Prophets are God's legal voice of authority on earth that God Himself has established for heaven. God chooses to speak to men, territories, systems, and realms in this world through prophecy. This is also the major reason why God chose to set prophets over nations (groups of people). God wants His voice over the people and prophets (and the prophetic) to carry His voice with a tremendous amount of creative ability. Remember, we just covered that the apostolic carries a tremendous fresh, new revelation.

Webster's Dictionary defines creation as: the act of bringing the world into ordered existence; the act of making, inventing, or producing as (a)—the act of investing with a new rank or office, or (b)—the first representation of a dramatic role. It goes on to clarify creation as: something that is created such as (a)—a world, (b)—creatures (singly or in aggregate), c—an original work of art, or (d)—a new (usually striking) article of clothing.

When God spoke the world into existence, that was a prophetic act—because He was creating! As He spoke the world into existence and the Holy Spirit was hovering over the face of the deep, that was a prophetic act—because He was creating! When God created us (mankind), that was a prophetic act—because He created us from a substance that DOES NOT have the ability to hold itself together, at least not without the prophetic! We were created from the dust of the earth, and it was God's prophetic breath that fused us to His prophetic word when He said, *"let Us make man in Our image and after Our likeness..."* and then man became a living soul or quickening fire (Genesis 1:26, 2:7).

This book is my prophetic piece of the truth. It is the revelation that my wife and I have been living from for over 20 years now. One day I was a drug addict and on my way to hell. From then, one divine prophetic encounter with God, not only was my soul saved from hell, but my life was changed forever! One day I was lost with no purpose. But then I received my salvation. I inherited the Kingdom of God and begin to rule and reign. Just two months later I was operating my own business. Why? God told me to start my own business! That is the power of the apostolic and prophetic.

Because of this creative power, not only have I created millions of dollars for my family and helped finance the Kingdom over the past 20 years, I have also changed the lives of thousands of people. I have made my industry better and have created millions of dollars for my clients as well. I started off as a gardener in the marketplace 20 years ago. Over the next six years of my life, I made over a million dollars cutting grass! It was during that season of my life that God was speaking to me about my future. Today I am a wealth strategist, an apostle, and a prophet of God who was given two messages. One is a burden to shift the church and the other is a message (word) to establish the Kingdom of God.

No Substitute for the Prophetic

Never forget that the prophetic can do things for you that nothing else can! There is no substitute for the prophetic at work in your life. You cannot transform society or take over in your industry, territory, city, or the world without it! You cannot advance in the Kingdom without the prophetic. Many who have tried to accomplish this without the prophetic have failed, or given up prematurely. Lack of the prophetic is one of the major reasons for divorce, bankruptcy, failure, debt, and the lack of influence and dominion in the *four-walled* church, in the marketplace, and in the work place among Christians and the body of Christ.

In the Old Testament, it was prophecy and the release of the prophetic which saved nations, shifted entire regions, and changed the course and direction of the church. Many lives were able to stay on the course, following the direction that God had for His people because of the prophetic. Nothing has changed today. The Old Testament was primarily written by prophets and the New Testament was primarily written by apostles—both are the foundation of the church (Ephesians 2:20).

The word prophetic is defined by Dr. Paula Price in *The Prophets Dictionary* as: the name given to predictive spheres of supernatural communications, acts, and influences from the spiritual world and its citizens; the ministry and work of the prophet; the disciplines and practices of revelation.

There are many things that will not be released until someone declares it prophetically. The prophetic word releases, activates, initiates, exhorts, comforts, shifts, establishes, changes, sets in order, and confirms. Prophetic utterances activate and release the plans and purposes of God. The prophetic word is predictive, but even more, it is creative. Prophets also carry a tremendous amount of authority.

The prophetic is designed to break open and take over whenever and where ever it is spoken, declared, or released! That could be in your life, ministry, business, finances, relationship, church, territory, industry, or anything else. Prophecy is a weapon against our enemy, Satan, and his entire kingdom! This is why you should NEVER despise (look down on) prophecy (1 Thessalonians 5:20). Currently, there is a revival that has broken out in Florida and that is great. I heard testimony from a person who recently attended a meeting in another state, and they told me how they laid out on the floor for four days, crying out to God for more. Listen, when it comes to prophecy and the prophetic, IT IS INSTANT and has NO DELAYS. This is why you should never despise it. Would you rather get revelation from God in an instant, or would you prefer to wait four days? When Jesus walked up to the 12 businessmen, and those in the marketplace and said, "Follow me," that was a prophetic word. They INSTANTLY responded—IMMEDIATELY they followed Him!

In Luke 9:57-62 Jesus said to "Launch out" into the deep. In other words, Jesus made a prophetic statement when He said, "I want you to launch out into the deep." Then, once they were in position, Jesus asked them to do something prophetic. He said to them, *"Let down your nets for a drought."* The first thing that Jesus showed these businessmen was that even though He was a carpenter, with the prophetic He had the ability **to create more wealth for them** in their

Through the prophetic, Jesus had the ability to create more wealth for them in one catch than they had ever done on their own!

business and with their partners in *one catch* then they had *ever done on their own*. When Simon Peter saw it (the prophetic act), he fell down at the feet of Jesus and he did not despise it (the prophetic).

In order to go INTO something you have to come OUT OF something, you have to leave something behind to accept something new! So, in order to go out into the deep, you first have to get off of the shore and leave behind the small things, the familiar areas, and even the comfortable relationships of people.

I can tell you where 75% of your problems originate. They come from the small-minded people in your life or from the non-prophetic people! It's amazing how others like to keep at least one struggling or dysfunctional person in their life, so on your worst day, you can always say, "At least I am not like so-and-so," or, "At least I haven't gone down *that* far yet!"

The apostolic and the prophetic will cause us to go somewhere that we have never been! The prophetic is a pioneering and a breakthrough anointing. As you open yourself up to the prophetic at work in your life, you will begin to totally go into NEW areas or arenas! Look at the following scripture:

This charge I commit unto thee, son Timothy, according to the prophecies which went before on thee, that thou by them mightest war a good warfare;

1 Timothy 1:18 KJV

99

The prophetic (and prophecy) is for war—so that your destiny can be fulfilled in the earth. This is why you should pray and speak prophetically.

God wants you and I to do something that has never, ever been done before on the earth or in the earth. Just as He did with men such as Adam, Noah, Abraham, Daniel, Enoch... This is why it is impossible for God to be a respector of persons.

Purpose of the Prophet

Prophecy is as relevant to the marketplace as it is from the pulpit—maybe more so. You may ask, "Why would God share something prophetic about the economy of the United States?" Well, unlike what many may portray that the duty of a prophet of Christ should be, a prophet is called like Abraham to become a blessing to the nations (Gen. 20:7). To bless means to invoke divine favor and protection. God wants to bless you and your family, and yes, He wants to raise up prophets in the marketplace that will impact every area of our world. This is not new revelation, this has always been the case. Study the scripture and you will find that God directed the economy, directed building projects, fought battles and stopped battles and impacted EVERY segment of society—for both believers and non-believers. Someone must go into the marketplace and into the work place and become the voice of God—and that someone is you! Will you join me on this journey? *(Source: Prophet Kim Clement)*

The Church has been in a process of restoration for the last 500 years. The apostles and prophets were the two ministries that God used to lay the foundation of the New Testament Church, and they will be the two who will bring completion to God's building, the Church. *(Source Dr. Bill Hamon, Bishop)*

All are not called to the office of a prophet, but everyone can and should be prophetic and everyone can and should prophesy (1 Corinthians 14:1, 31).

In Luke 11:49, Jesus said that He would send the people prophets and apostles. In Ephesians 4:8, Jesus gave gifts to men and one of them was the ministry office of the prophet.

1 Corinthians 12:28 says, *"And God has set some in the church, first apostles, secondarily prophets, thirdly teachers, after that miracles, then gifts of healings, helps, governments (administrators/systems), diversity of tongues (ability to speak every man's language)."* This reference to tongues is the same as the day of Pentecost, when those present were able to speak in recognizable languages that they had not learned. This was the result of a supernatural manifestation.

Our Words Frame Our World!

There are some things that cannot and will not take place until AFTER they have been prophesied (or prophetically released), spoken, and decreed. Along with this prophetic declaration comes everything that is needed or necessary to bring that word to pass. Fulfillment is released within that prophetic word. In other words, the ability and creative force is within the release of the word so that there is nothing natural that can stop you—not inexperience, not time, not culture, not lack of resources, nothing! That word is coming directly from heaven when it is spoken by (or through) a true prophet or prophetic person!

Prophetic Teaching

Prophetic teaching is necessary to the success and future of every believer. Unfortunately, most *four-walled* churches spend more time preaching—which primarily inspires and stimulates your emotions. In fact, what we actually need is prophetic and apostolic teaching which feeds the spirit and activates destiny. There is a huge difference between preaching and teaching and prophetic and apostolic teaching and preaching. The latter releases the apostolic and the prophetic.

Prophetic gatherings are times of impartation, refreshing, activation, release, and revelation. There is a corporate anointing that comes when prophets and prophetic people gather for worship, prayer, teaching, and utterance that causes believers to come to a higher level (1 Samuel 10:6). My wife and I have led a weekly prophetic gathering for over 14 months now, and have seen tremendous results in the life of the people that have gathered. (For more information, visit www.PropheticGathering.com).

Prophetic gatherings can be times of personal prophecy, corporate prophecy, prophetic teaching, or even a prophetic presbytery. Apostolic churches (apostolic people) should have prophetic gatherings which will be times of refreshing (Acts 3:19). Prophetic gatherings help believers get released into their inheritance (Genesis 49). *(Source: Dr. Paula Price, The Prophets Dictionary)*

Reformation always requires new teaching and a restructuring of thought patterns. Prophetic teaching helps release the apostolic. Once you are convinced that what is being done is scriptural, you can confidently embrace that what is being built is also scriptural. Prophetic teaching exposes the false concepts and foundations (even those that were well-intentioned) that previous church leaders have built upon in the past. *(Source: Apostle John Eckhardt, LeaderShift)*

Let's take a look at several scriptures that we can identify for prophetic and apostolic preaching and teaching.

For the kingdom of God is not in word, but in power.

I Corinthians 4:20

For I will not dare to speak of any of those things which Christ hath not wrought by me, to make the Gentiles obedient, by word and deed.

Romans 15:18

Long time therefore abode they speaking boldly in the Lord, which gave testimony unto the word of his grace, and granted signs and wonders to be done by their hands.

Acts 14:3

Through mighty signs and wonders, by the power of the Spirit of God; so that from Jerusalem, and round about unto Illyricum, I have fully preached the gospel of Christ.

Romans 15:19

Truly the signs of an apostle were wrought among you in all patience, in signs, and wonders, and mighty deeds.

2 Corinthians 12:12

For our gospel came not unto you in word only, but also in power, and in the

*Holy Ghost, and in much assurance;
as you know what manner of men
we were among you for your sake.*

1 Thessalonians 1:5

*In the kingdom there is neither Jew
nor Greek, there is neither bond nor
free, there is neither male nor female:
for ye are all one in Christ Jesus.*

Galatians 3:28

*And I will give you pastors according
to mine heart, which shall feed you
with knowledge and understanding.*

Jeremiah 3:15

*And I will set up shepherds over them
which shall feed them: and they shall
fear no more, nor be dismayed, neither
shall they be lacking, saith the LORD.*

Jeremiah 23:4

Preaching the gospel of the kingdom...

Matthew 4:23-25

Signs and wonders...
Kingdom is everlasting.

Daniel 4:3

I have preached righteousness in
the great congregation...

Psalms 40:9,10

God never intended for denominations or religious organizations to rule the earth. God intended for YOU, THE BELIEVER, HIS SONS, and DAUGHTERS to have dominion—to rule and to reign in the earth!

And God said, Let us (Father, Son,
and Holy Spirit) make man (mankind)
in our image, after our likeness and
let them have comlete authority...

Genesis 1:26 AMP

This is the main reason for STRONG apostolic and prophetic teaching. It releases and reveals to you that YOU are created in the EXACT IMAGE of GOD, and that YOU have been given the authority and the ability to do GREATER WORKS! Not similar works, but the same works, and even greater works (John 14:12).

Obey and Prosper

Believe in the Lord your God, so shall you be established; believe his prophets, so shall you prosper.

2 Chronicles 20:20

The Greek word for prosper is TSALACH, and means to push forward, break out, go over, and be profitable. It is not enough to just believe in the prophet's ministry and mantle, or in the prophetic, but you must also OBEY what the prohet says and heed the instructions of what is said! Not embracing or obeying what a prophet says can not only cost you EVERYTHING, it can also cost you your very life. Failure to obey was the reason why the children of Israel wandered in the wilderness for 40 years, and why many died within a few miles of the Promised Land. Only two people from their generation were able to live, and cross over the Jordan River into the Promised Land. These were Joshua and Caleb—the two that had obeyed the prophet's ministry (Moses) and had a prophetic report to bring back as the prophet (Moses) had asked them to do (Numbers 13:1-33). They didn't just believe, they also obeyed!

Prophets are placed side by side with the apostles as the foundation of the New Testament Church (Ephesians 2:20). It is clear that what really characterized the prophet was immediate communion with

God, a divine communication of what the prophet had to declare. Two things are necessary for a prophet; an insight granted by God into the divine secrets or mysteries, and a communication to others of these secrets. It is my prophetic desire that I am able to grant you access into the secrets and mysteries that will give you and grant you access into the Kingdom of God until you "Master the Combination for Kingdom and Global Dominance of All World Systems!"

One prophetic word can launch you to the next level— The same result could take years to achieve in the natural.

One prophetic word can launch or accelerate you from one place to the next in an instant. In the natural, without a prophetic word, the same result could take years to accomplish. Saul was changed, immediately turned into another man as he was coming down the mountain when he came in contact with the prophetic company (1 Samuel 10:6).

It is important that you know who you meet along the way in your life—especially apostles and prophets. Why? Because they carry the necessary "upgrade" that you need to accelerate you toward your destiny.

Every apostle needs a prophet. Every prophet needs an apostle. Every king (business person or entrepreneur) needs a prophet, and every *four-walled* church leader or pastor needs all three.

The Prophet's Reward is a "Profit" Reward

Everything that you and I will ever need is already present and is located in one of two places!

- One: It is already inside of you (placed there long before time ever began).

- Two: It is right around you (within your circle, your reach, your region, or your resources).

Everything and everyone that Jesus needed when He started his ministry was right around him, and it is no different with you. Right now, today the Kingdom of Heaven is at hand or within hand's reach. Remember what God told Joshua? *"Every place that the sole of your feet shall walk on, that have I already given to you"* (Joshua 1:3).

In 2 Corinthians 4:7, Jesus said that this treasure has been hidden in earthen vessels. In 1 Corinthians 2:6, we learn that eyes have not seen, and ears have not yet heard the things which God has prepared for them that love Him.

Whatever you need is available to you through the prophetic!

- ○ UNKNOWN—will become KNOWN
- ○ HIDDEN—will become SEEN
- ○ MYSTERIES—will be REVEALED
- ○ SECRETS—will be HEARD

The things of God are not hidden from you, but for you!

He that receiveth you receiveth Me, and He that receiveth Me receiveth Him that sent Me. He that receiveth a prophet in the Name of a Prophet shall receive a prophet's reward; and he that receiveth a righteous man in the Name of a Righteous Man shall receive a righteous man's reward. And whosoever shall give to drink unto one of these little ones a cup of cold water only in the Name of a Disciple, verily I say unto you, he shall in no wise lose his reward.

Matthew 10:40-42

The secret things belong to the Lord, but that which he reveals belongs to us!

Deuteronomy 29:9,29

*In the house of the righteous is much treasure:
but in the revenues of the wicked is trouble.*

Proverbs 15:6

*I am made a minister of this
dispensation ... the mystery of which
hath been hid from ages...*

Colossians 1:25-26

*For nothing is secret, that shall not be
made manifest; neither any thing hid, that
shall not be known and come abroad.*

Luke 8:17

*Which in other ages (previous generation)
was not made known unto the sons of
men, as it is now revealed unto his holy
apostles and prophets by the Spirit;*

Ephesians 3:5

Prophecy releases you into your wealth! It's not enough to just be prosperous—you must become wealthy!

- ○ Poverty: a mental state
- ○ Prosperity: a condition, mindset or position
- ○ Wealth: accumulation of goods, income streams, something that can not be cut off.

This is why you bless the prophets (bless them financially, bless them with words, bless them with your fruitfulness)! God sends prophets to you because He wants to prosper you!

You must believe the prophets—you must obey the word of the Lord that comes through them. This provides you with a measure of faith for the things around you (Hebrews 11:6). It also provides you with a measure of grace for the gifts that are already inside of you (Ephesians 4:7).

The Prophetic Will Break the Barriers (or Limits) Off of Six Areas of Your Life!

Six is the number of man. It represents flesh. Once these barriers (of the flesh) have been broken, you can then begin to prosper so that you can become wealthy!

As you invested (financially) in purchasing this book, and as you invest (your time and energy) in reading and studying this book, I am prophetically releasing multiplication into six areas of your life. These areas are going to become limitless for you, your family, your life, your business, and your ministry!

- **ONE: YOUR CONFESSION** (you will speak from a heavenly place while on earth, and whatever you speak or decree will have no more delay)

- **TWO: YOUR IDENTITY** (you no longer have to think like a person that is bound by their culture, but instead you will realize that you get to act with the authority of God on the earth)

- THREE: **YOUR BUSINESS** (you will see an increase in what you are being paid—you will begin to be paid for what you know and not just for what you do with what you know)

- FOUR: **YOUR LANGUAGE** (you will be able to speak everyone's language so that they understand you and will respond to you, your product, or your message)

- FIVE: **FORGIVENESS OF SINS** (you will experience total forgiveness from your past mistakes, failures, or short comings)

- SIX: **YOUR VISION** (you will receive fresh vision for wealth creation, for the Kingdom, and for the next generation)

The blessing of the Lord, it maketh rich,
and He addeth no sorrow with it.

Proverbs 10:22

Before you can crack the apostolic and prophetic code, you must embrace an apostolic and prophetic paradigm.

ॐ ☙

CHAPTER SIX

THE APOSTOLIC AND PROPHETIC CODE

ॐ ☙

We have established that there are mysteries in the Kingdom which can only be known by revelation. I want to be very clear that the apostolic and prophetic code is not a doctrine, but a revealed prophetic word that will cause you to go somewhere that you have never been before! As I was seeking the Lord about my calling and how I could fulfill my purpose in the earth, He began to show me many things. As I searched them out, God began to show me patterns, systems, and numbers which, as they were revealed, turned out to be a code. As these patterns became more clear, I was reminded of the movie, "The Matrix." As I continued to search and study, it was as if the numbers were coming down on a screen and suddenly made sense. I realized that if I understood the code, then unlocking the mystery became possible. I want to share this revelation, this code with you so that the message can become clear for your life. This code (or my revelation) will unlock the mysteries (gifts & callings) that God Himself placed inside of you before time began.

What is a Code?

Webster's Dictionary defines *code* as: a systematic statement of a body of law, especially one given statutory force; a system of principles or rules (a moral code); a system of signals or symbols for communication; a system of symbols (such as letters or numbers) used to represent assigned and often secret meanings; a set of instructions.

Have you ever seen a video stream online? Normally, it appears as a still picture with a small button or arrow that you click on in order to activate it. When you click, the video stream begins—it is literally like watching TV on the web. It seems simple, right? All you have to do is press a button. But, in order for the stream to be viewed, several things must happen to prepare the video. First, the programmer must know the programming. He must be able to create a code so that the video can be embedded on the correct page and location of the website so a person will be able to access and view it. Second, the video must be placed in a source file on the website's server so that it can stream from that source whenever the file is accessed. So, even though it seems simple, the process is actually quite complex.

In much the same way, if we are going to be able to take over all of the world's systems we must first understand the programming—that is, we must have a clear and biblical view of the present day Kingdom of God like the early apostles did in Jesus' day. Then, we must be plugged in to our source file. Our source of power and authority comes from the apostolic and the prophetic. It is accessed when we embrace the ministry office gifts of apostle and prophet and as we are in direct covenant relationships with them. It is not enough to just hear them preach from the pulpit of the local *four-walled* church.

You and I have already been PRE-WIRED to succeed! In order to step fully into our calling and access our destiny, we must step out of the four walls of the church, step past the three gates of hell (religion, tradition, and racism) and step through the three gates of heaven (the *ecclesia* (*four-walled* church), the marketplace, and the work place). Then, we must be directly connected (wired) to apostles and prophets in this present day. Even more importantly, we must be specifically connected (wired) to their revelation!

There are codes (gifts and callings) that God Himself put inside of you that only certain individuals can activate. This is the reason God said that He would send you apostles, prophets, and shepherds (apostolic leaders) that could feed you. This is also why when Jesus ascended on high, He gave gifts unto men (Ephesians 4).

When God Almighty created us, He ENCODED us in HIS IMAGE and LIKENESS—encoded us to have dominion on the earth! When Jesus came to earth and released the Kingdom of Heaven, He activated that same code again, right where we left off in the garden, when Adam failed after falling into sin. This code enables us now (as it did Adam, then) to SUBDUE the earth and to have dominion over all flesh, and to multiply. Isaiah 54:2-3 and Psalms 19:4 tells us to enlarge our borders (our house, the place of our tent) and to increase our line.

The apostolic and prophetic code is the master combination for global dominance of all world systems by the Kingdom of Heaven. The Kingdom of Heaven (seen) and the Kingdom of God (unseen) encompasses all (both the earthly realm and the heavenly realm), and are synonymous.

It is Your Legal Right to Rule!

The heaven, even the heavens, are the Lords: but the earth hath He given to the children of men.

Psalms 115:16

This is one of my favorite Scriptures in the Bible. My question to you is this: what are you going to do with the piece of earth (territory) that God has given you to rule and reign on? The longer you are out of place, the longer the kingdom of darkness gets to rule in your stead. Jesus told Peter, *"And I will give unto thee the keys (access) of the kingdom of heaven: and whatsoever thou shalt bind (permit) on earth shall be bound (permitted) in heaven: and whatsoever thou shalt loose (establish) on earth shall be loosed (established) in heaven"* (Matthew 16:19). This was a prophetic statement to those that were (and are) in the marketplace and have a revelation not just of who Christ is, but more so to those who understand that they are to do the same apostolic and prophetic work that God Himself has revealed to those that are connected to the Kingdom of God on earth.

Revelation Released and Mysteries Revealed

It is important to understand that although preaching has an important role to play, it is going to take a prophetic revelation to obtain the mysteries of the Kingdom. Look what the religious leaders asked Jesus in Luke 17:20-21, "And when He was demanded of the Pharisees, when the Kingdom of God should come, He answered them and said, 'The Kingdom of God cometh not with observation: Neither shall they say, Lo here! or, lo there! for, behold, the KINGDOM OF GOD

IS WITHIN YOU.'" In other words, the Pharisees were looking for an outward sign of the Kingdom when it was standing right in front of them! Jesus told them that not only is the Kingdom of God near you, it is WITHIN you! This is an illustration of why we need to be taught, and not just preached at. Preaching CAN NOT release revelation or reveal mysteries. Revelation comes directly from heaven.

Preaching elevates, inspires, encourages, instructs, and provides information. Prophecy (prophetic and apostolic teaching) imparts, reveals, activates, shifts you in or out of something, and establishes you. It will take apostolic strategies and prophetic impartation to activate God's plan for your life. The only way you

It will take apostolic strategies and prophetic impartation to activate God's plan for your life.

can take over is if you first possess the Kingdom of God. The Kingdom of Heaven is now, in your lifetime. You must embrace who you are in Christ and then train and raise up the next generation of leaders—your sons and daughters! Understand this—our realms (world) are framed by our words; and prophetic words have power. In order to understand the Master's pattern and follow His plan, prophetic keys, prophetic instructions, and apostolic directions are required.

"For our gospel (Kingdom message) came not unto you in word (preaching) only, but also in power, and in the Holy Ghost, and in much assurance; as you know what manner of men were among you for your sake."

1 Thessalonians 1:5

We have a GREAT DESTINY to fulfill. The Kingdom of God is an invisible Kingdom, and we rule and reign from a spiritual or heavenly position. To be prepared, we need strong apostolic and prophetic preaching and teaching that comes from apostles and prophets who have power, have the Holy Ghost, and have much assurance.

The Master (or Master's) Combination

The "Master Combination" or, the "Master's Combination" was created purposefully. Jesus selected twelve non-church men—men who were not church leaders, but were businessmen, even considered heathens, to take over the world, its systems and society! Not 1,200 men, not 12,000 and not 12 million. His pattern was to create a team of like-minded, world changers that were from the marketplace and the work place. He chose men that possessed an entrepreneurial spirit with an unlimited mindset for total success. His perfect pattern is still the same today. His disciples (the twelve apostles) were not functioning inside the *four-walled*, established church as "ministers." So, if you feel called outside of the *four-walled* church, realize that Jesus wants to release the apostolic and prophetic combination so that you can crack the apostolic and the prophetic code within you.

What is a Combination?

Webster's defines *combination* as: a result or product of combining, especially an alliance of individuals, corporations, or states united to achieve a social, political, or economic end; two or more persons working as a team; an ordered sequence (such as a sequence of letters or numbers chosen in setting a lock). It is also defined as: the mechanism operating or moved by the sequence; any subset of a set considered without regard to order within the subset; an instrument designed to perform two or more tasks; the act or process of combining (especially that of uniting to form a chemical compound).

Remember what Jesus said in Luke 8:10. *"For you it is given to know the mysteries of the Kingdom of God: but to others in parables (outside of the Kingdom); that seeing they might not see, and hearing*

they might not understand." Do you know that others can also mean Christians or church members? This
means anyone living outside of the Kingdom (outside
of its rights, its privileges, and authority)! If you don't
understand how the Kingdom really works, or if you
think that it is somewhere out in the future and not
here NOW, actually in your hands, then you will have
a hard time operating in it!

There is a reason why Jesus picked twelve men outside of the *four-walled* church of His day. He chose
them from the world, and then boldly told them to
stop what they were doing and follow Him into the
Kingdom. These men obeyed immediately, but the
four-walled church leaders only asked Him a lot of
questions. They challenged His motives, His methods
and even the company that He kept. These men (the
others) didn't understand the meaning of His words
or the intent of His message. So, the *four-walled*
church leaders of Jesus' day COULD NOT comprehend his apostolic and prophetic commands. Why?
Because they were bound up by religion, tradition,
and racism. This is fascinating! This is refreshing to
me—those who were in the marketplace and in the
work place COULD understand the command (Jesus'
apostolic and prophetic instructions). They were able
to obey the commands and instructions, and were
thus able to endure all types of affliction, persecution, rejection, abandonment, isolation, death, and
even the Lord's crucifixion. When their time came

to rule and reign, THOSE THAT WERE IN THE MAR-
KETPLACE AND WORK PLACE were able to turn their
known world UPSIDE DOWN! Today, those of you who
can and will embrace the message and revelation of
this book will be charged to embrace the ministry of
apostles and prophets as well as the apostolic and the
prophetic. Then and only then will we be able to turn
OUR WORLD right-side up (which is established on the
foundation of the apostles and prophets)! Now THAT
is the New Testament Church!

What is a Pattern?

Webster's defines *pattern* as: a form or model pro-
posed for imitation; something designed or used as
a model for making things (such as a dressmaker's
pattern); an artistic, musical, literary, or mechani-
cal design or form; a natural or chance configuration;
the distribution of shrapnel, bombs on a target, or
shot from a shotgun; the grouping made on a target
by bullets; a reliable sample of traits, acts, tenden-
cies, or other observable characteristics of a person,
group, or institution (such as a behavior pattern or
spending pattern). It is further defined as: the flight
path prescribed for an airplane that is coming in for a
landing; a prescribed route to be followed by a pass
receiver in football; a discernible, coherent system
based on the intended interrelationship of compo-
nent parts (such as a foreign policy pattern); frequent
or widespread incidence (such as a pattern of dissent
or a pattern of violence).

Jesus established a pattern when He asked His disciples to do something that other men had never done before. Look at this passage:

Jesus sent out these Twelve, charging them,...and as you go, preach, saying, "The Kingdom of Heaven is at hand!" Cure the sick, raise the dead, cleanse the lepers, drive out demons...Behold, I am sending you out like sheep in the midst of wolves; be wary and wise as serpents, and be innocent (harmless, guileless, and without falsity) as doves. [Gen 3:1.] Be on guard against men [whose way or nature is to act in opposition to God]; for they will deliver you up to councils and flog you in their synagogues, And you will be brought before governors and kings for My sake, as a witness to bear testimony before them and to the Gentiles (the nations).

Matthew 10:5-18 AMP

I am told that in order to get an airplane off of the ground and up into the air, it must go at full speed. Once the plane reaches the right altitude, the pilot can pull back on the throttle and begin to fly at a normal cruising speed. They say that half of their fuel is consumed just to get up and off the ground, but in order to achieve flight, all pilots must follow this same pattern. If not, they will not only run out of fuel, but they will never get to their desired destination. If a pilot deviates from the pattern, he could lose his own life and as well as the lives of all his passengers.

Just like an airplane trying to take off, so are you with this book and revelation. If you do not go at full speed and give it everything you have from the beginning, you may go up and down the runway, but you will never get off the ground. If you don't embrace revelation whole-heartedly and IMMEDIATELY begin to run with it, YOU WILL NEVER LEAVE the runway of average, yesterday, or routine. The gates of religion, tradition, and racism are stronger in their hold on you, than the force of gravity is on an airplane. But, I believe in you. I believe that you will shift and grab hold of the Kingdom and do great and mighty things. He whom the Son has set free, is free indeed (John 8:36)!

When Jesus came out of the wilderness announcing, *"Repent, for the Kingdom of Heaven is at hand, FOLLOW ME!"* They literally left what they were doing. Because of their obedience, INFLUENCE, POWER, and STRENGTH to ADVANCE in the Kingdom came on them from heaven! If we (as Kingdom Representatives) are going to take our rightful place in the marketplace, we must also follow the same patterns that Jesus demonstrated and released.

Our Charge

Just as Jesus sent out His apostles during His earthly ministry, He is sending us out now as apostles and prophets with the same apostolic and prophetic spirit to penetrate every region, every industry, and every realm. He charges us to preach that the Kingdom of Heaven is at hand. Remember, that the Kingdom of Heaven is not just near you, it is IN you. This means that Jesus Christ has placed apostolic and prophetic ability within you so that YOU can change the world—now go!

Jesus has given you the authority to cure the sick, raise the dead, cleanse the lepers, and drive out demons. He warns you to be on your guard; that you are like sheep in the midst of wolves. The strongholds of religion, tradition, and racism will come against you and stand in opposition to you. They will try to murder you and control you. But you can respond just like Paul did. *"When Paul had gathered a bundle of sticks and laid them on the fire, there came a viper out of the heat, and fastened on his hand"* (Acts 28:1-7). Paul's response to the attack was to just SHAKE IT OFF! And you can do the same! Now that you have embraced the apostolic and the prophetic, now that you know it is your time to rule and reign in

Shake it off!

the marketplace and in the work place, you can shake off the venomous attacks. Things that you have had to tolerate in the past, you now will have the necessary strength, power, and grace to just shake off!

Jesus goes on to encourage you even more. Not only will you be able to withstand attacks from the enemy and from others, but for His sake and in order to bear His testimony, you will be brought before governors and kings! This is good news. This indicates His confidence in you and demonstrates His trust. He would not send you before governors and kings without anointing you and establishing your dominion and authority as His voice as a Kingdom Representative to them!

I want you to say this out loud:

"I AM A KINGDOM REPRESENTATIVE. I WAS STRATEGICALLY PLACED ON EARTH RIGHT NOW TO REPRESENT HEAVEN. I AM GOD'S APOSTLE, PROPHET, AND KING IN THE EARTH SO THAT THE CHURCH OF JESUS CHRIST WILL BE ESTABLISHED. NOW THAT I POSSESS THE KINGDOM AND WITH THE APOSTOLIC AND THE

PROPHETIC OPERATING EVERY DAY IN MY LIFE, MY MINISTRY, MY FINANCES, AND MY BUSINESS, ALL MYSTERIES AND SECRETS THAT HAVE NEVER BEEN KNOWN TO MAN BEFORE (EVEN IN PREVIOUS GENERATIONS) ARE NOW BEING MADE KNOWN AND REVEALED TO ME. I CAN DO SOMETHING THAT NO OTHER MAN (NO OTHER GENERATION) HAS EVER DONE BEFORE IN THE EARTH. I WAS CREATED TO RULE AND REIGN. I WAS CREATED TO CREATE WEALTH!

By the Numbers

When I began searching the Scriptures, numbers began to fall into place. The more I studied, the more significant revelation began to be associated with these numbers. As we explore the numbers further, it is important to realize that throughout history, many things we will talk about have already taken place. However, they have never occurred simultaneously. This is a very exciting time. As you know, 2008 is the year of RELEASED or OPENED GATES! It's about your role and your rights! What you couldn't do before (for whatever reason) YOU CAN DO IT NOW! The apostle's office was the last office to be re-established, and now that it has been fully restored in the earth, the hand of God can go out and grab hold of the world and all of its systems through YOU, YOUR LIFE, YOUR BUSINESS and YOUR MINISTRY. The pieces are all in place. All five offices (along with all of the necessary grace and its abilities) are now fully restored—apostle, prophet, evangelist, pastor, and teacher (which is the hand of God). The glory of the Lord is unfolding and His plan is being revealed through his holy apostles and prophets.

Now, let's look at some numbers. Then, after we have gone through each number and where it comes from, I will tie them all together for you, revealing the apostolic and prophetic code that unlocks the mysteries of God. This is not meant to be an exhaustive study, nor is it meant to be something "spooky" or "extra-spiritual." However, I do want to take you to a revelatory place that you have never been before so that you can see something and do something great in the earth that has never been done before.

The code consists of numbers and patterns that I will first introduce, and then I will break them down individually. The name of this book is: *Cracking the Apostolic & Prophetic Code—The Master Combination for Kingdom and Global Dominance of ALL the World Systems!* The purpose of this book is to reveal, to impart, to activate, to shift, and to release apostolic and prophetic strategies and insight for the present day Church on how you can take over, influence, or transform your family, region, territory, culture, city, industry, state, country ,and world!

The Code

The Code consists of numbers and groupings of numbers that have prophetic significance.

$$12 + 27 + 5 + 3 = 47$$

$$47 = 40 + 7$$

$$40 + 7 + 3 = 50$$

We'll begin with the first number in the code—twelve. Don't worry, it will all make sense and tie together at the end. Then, the prophetic and apostolic light will come on inside of you like never before. This will cause fresh revelation to be revealed to you so that the Kingdom (and living in the Kingdom) will no longer be a mystery. You will see that the Kingdom of Heaven and the Kingdom of God is in you, and that God has put the Kingdom (and the responsibility of it) in your hands. We are created to rule and reign with it!

The Number Twelve

Twelve is a perfect number. It signifies perfection of government, or governmental perfection. Twelve is also a multiple found in all numbers that pertain to rulership. The sun which "rules" the day, and the moon and stars which "govern" the night, do so by their passage through the twelve signs of the Zodiac which completes the great circle of the heavens of 360 (12 x 30) degrees or divisions, and thus governs the year.

There are a total of 164 Scriptures in the Bible that deal with the number twelve. Let's look at some of them.

Twelve Patriarchs

There were twelve patriarchs from Seth to Noah and his family. There were twelve patriarchs from Shem to Jacob.

The Temple of Solomon

The Temple of Solomon has the number twelve as the predominating factor. This is in contrast with the Tabernacle, which had the number five. This fact agrees with and demonstrates the grace which shines in the Tabernacle, and the glory of the Kingdom which is displayed in the Temple.

When we come to the New Testament, we find the same great principle pervading the apostolic government that we see in the patriarchal and national government. We have:

○ *twelve* apostles

○ *twelve* foundations in the heavenly Jerusalem

○ *twelve* gates

○ *twelve* pearls

○ *twelve* angels

Twelve Years

Jesus was twelve years old when He first appears in public (Luke 2:42) and utters His first recorded words.

Twelve Legions

Twelve legions of angels mark the perfection of angelic powers (Matt 26:53).

"For unto us a child is born, unto us a son is given: and the government shall be upon his shoulder: and his name shall be called Wonderful, Counselor, The Mighty God, The Everlasting Father, The Prince of Peace.

Of the increase of his government and peace there shall be no end, upon the throne of David, and upon his kingdom, to order it, and to establish it with judgment and with justice from henceforth even for ever. The zeal of the LORD of hosts will perform this.

Isaiah 9:6-7

The spiritual meaning of shoulder is all power. Webster's defines *shoulders* as: capacity for bearing a task or blame (placed the guilt squarely on his shoulders; an area adjacent to or along the edge of a higher, more prominent, or more important part.

There are twelve Kingdoms present on the earth, and each of these twelve realms (worlds) is meant to be under the dominion and authority of Christ through the life of every saint (or believer) in the marketplace and work place as an apostle or prophet, or with the apostolic and the prophetic function.

Let's take a look at some very important Scriptures:

"Again, the devil taketh Him up into an exceeding high mountain, and sheweth Him all the kingdoms of the world, and the glory of them; And saith unto Him, All these things will I give thee, if thou

wilt fall down and worship me."
Matthew 4:8-9

"I am He that liveth, and was dead; and,
behold, I am alive for evermore, Amen;
and have the keys of hell and of death."
Revelations 1:18

"I will give unto thee the keys of the
kingdom of heaven: and whatsoever thou
shalt bind on earth shall be bound in
heaven: and whatsoever thou shalt loose
on earth shall be loosed in heaven."
Matthew 16:19

"Fear not, little flock; for it is your Father's
good pleasure to give you the kingdom."
Luke 12:32

"But the saints of the most High shall
take the kingdom, and possess the
kingdom for ever, even for ever and ever.

Until the Ancient of days came, and
judgment was given to the saints of
the most High; and the time came that
the saints possessed the kingdom.

And the kingdom and dominion, and the greatness of the kingdom under the whole heaven, shall be given to the people of the saints of the most High, whose kingdom is an everlasting kingdom, and all dominions shall serve and obey Him."

Daniel 7:18,22,and 27

"And the seventh angel sounded; and there were great voices in heaven, saying, The kingdoms of this world are become the kingdoms of our Lord, and of his Christ; and he shall reign for ever and ever. "

Revelation 11:15

"And I will overthrow the throne of kingdoms, and I will destroy the strength of the kingdoms of the heathen; and I will overthrow the chariots, and those that ride in them; and the horses and their riders shall come down, every one by the sword of his brother."

Haggai 2:22

And in the days of these kings shall the God of heaven set up a kingdom, which shall never be destroyed: and the kingdom shall not be left to other people, but it shall break in pieces and consume all these kingdoms, and it shall stand for ever.

Daniel 2:44

The Kingdom

The Kingdom of God always starts with Jesus which then connects you to the Holy Ghost (who is the God-head on earth). The Holy Ghost then connects to the sons and daughters of God who have been given the authority on the earth with POWER. Once you have been given POWER (God-like ability), you are to go and do GOOD. You are to heal ALL that are oppressed of the devil (outside of the Kingdom). YOU have the POWER to bring them INTO THE KINGDOM, because God is WITH YOU (Acts 10:38), because THE KINGDOM OF HEAVEN IS AT HAND!

In order to heal those that are OPPRESSED, you must first become POSSESSED with the Kingdom!

So far, here is the best definition of the Kingdom of God that I have been able to find and he calls it a "working definition" which means that it is changeable, not perfect or final. It is not a political adminis-tration, a geographic territory, or an abstract notion. However, it is a rule. It does have a realm and it is a pragmatic and dynamic reality. Simply defined, the Kingdom of God is:

> *The sphere of God's will, reign, and rule. It is located throughout heaven and the cos-mos, and wherever on earth the manifes-tation of his sovereignty, holiness, power, and kingly authority is acknowledged and obeyed. That means it is realized both in-ternally and externally, within and among, to draw human hearts to Him, to bless and discipline his people, and to defeat his ene-mies. It is to be entered, exercised, and ad-vanced by every Christian who follows Jesus, and experienced in every aspect of society. However, it is not universally recognized, is contested, opposed and persecuted, and is greatly under-realized.*

John Noe, Ph.D.,
Restoring the Kingdom-of-God Worldview to the
Church and the World

The Twelve Kingdoms

Let's get one thing straight before we move on. Even though we rule first from a heavenly realm or from a position of heaven, once we receive this revelation and know that the Kingdom of Heaven is in our hands, we are to RULE and REIGN on this EARTH. This is literal—on this planet, this physical place called earth! **There are twelve Kingdoms (realms or worlds). They are:**

Education	*Government*	*Technology*
Financial	*Social*	*Medicine*
Entertainment	*Media*	*Internet*
Real Estate	*Culture*	*Invention*

Christians (believers and the saints of the Most High God) are meant to rule and reign in each of these twelve realms as Kings or Kingdom Representatives on the earth. Access to each realm (Kingdom) is open for us through one of the three gates of heaven discussed earlier; the *ecclesia* (Church), the marketplace, or the work place. This is why it is SO IMPORTANT for us to understand WHICH GATE we are called to and WHAT REALMS (Kingdoms) we have been authorized by God to exercise dominion over.

Conversely, access to these realms (Kingdoms) is blocked by one of the three gates of hell discussed earlier; religion, tradition, or racism. This is why you MUST be completely delivered and free from these demonic strongholds and able to walk confidently in your anointing (just as the King of Kings did) as a king yourself and be set in your place. Why did the Lord say that He would send you apostles and prophets? Because most *four-walled* church leaders or pastors won't release kings out into the Kingdom in the marketplace and work place. It isn't their nature. Their nature is to manage people (steward or herd them). The nature and anointing of apostles and prophets is to release and send people out for governmental assignment to rule, reign, and take over!

Below is a brief overview of the 12 Kingdoms (realms or worlds). It is not meant to be an exhaustive study. Most of the information and definitions were gathered and adapted from www.wikipedia.org.

1. Education

Education is the realm of knowledge which shapes and changes. Education encompasses teaching as well as learning knowledge, proper conduct, and technical competency. Education focuses on the cultivation of skills, trades, or professions, as well as mental, moral, and aesthetic development.

2. Government

Government is the realm of politics, the military and religion. There are different layers or levels of government: local, regional, and national. A government is defined as "the organization, that is the governing authority of a political unit; the ruling power in a political society; and the apparatus through which a governing body functions and exercises authority." Government has the authority to make and enforce laws, to levy taxes, to adjudicate disputes, and to issue administrative decisions. Government maintains the peace of communal life through the use of authorized force when and where it fails to persuade. Society relies on government to establish and enforce laws so that personal freedoms can be maintained and the economy can thrive. True, personal autonomy must be constrained within our communities—this is necessary to keep the rights of one from infringing on the rights of another.

3. Technology

Technology is a vast realm that is difficult to define, but put simply it is comprised of software and systems. Technology is a broad concept that deals with our knowledge and application of tools and crafts. It affects society's ability to control and adapt to its environment. In modern society, technology is a consequence of science and engineering, although several technological advances predate the two concepts. Technology can refer to the material objects we use such as machines, hardware, or utensils. But it can also encompass broader themes including systems, methods of organization, and techniques. The term can either be applied generally or to specific areas. Examples would include fields like construction technology, medical technology, or computer technology.

4. Financial (Economics)

Finance encompasses everything from insurance, banking and investments, to the Stock Market, the Futures Market, and the Forex Market. It touches entrepreneurs and business, capitol and assets, and extends all the way to the broad concepts of money and wealth. The field of finance refers to the concepts of time, money, and risk, and how they are interrelated. The term "finance" may thus incorporate any of the following: the study of money and other assets, the management and control of those assets, profiling and managing project risks, the science of managing money, the industry that delivers financial services. When used as a verb, "to finance" means to provide funds for business or for an individual's large purchases (car, home, etc.). Economics is the social science that studies the production, distribution, and consumption of goods and services. An economic system is a set of methods and standards by which a society decides and organizes the ownership and allocation of economic resources. An economic system is a system that involves the production, distribution, and consumption of goods and services between the entities in a particular society.

5. Social (Society)

The social realm is comprised of the environment we live in, it may be country clubs or community parks, local chambers of commerce and city councils, "old" money or "new" money, projects or gated/estate neighborhoods. It includes charities and non-profit groups, art and museums, families and nations. It is broad. A society is a grouping of individuals characterized by patterns of relationships between them that may have distinctive culture and institutions, or, more broadly, an economic, social, and industrial infrastructure in which a varied multitude of people or peoples are a part. Members of a society may be from different ethnic groups such as Hispanic or Native American. A society may be a particular people, such as the Saxons; a nation state, such as Bhutan; or even a broader cultural group, such as a Western society.

Society often represents a sub-culture within a broader culture. It is commonly a grouping of individuals which is characterized by common interests such as; soccer moms, union members, fraternities or sororities, golfers, etc. Society may also refer to groups such as; the rich and famous, or an association that exists to promote an academic discipline. A subset of society may be a university, a student club, etc. The word society may also refer to an organized voluntary association of people for religious, benevolent, cultural, scientific, political, patriotic, or other purpose such as the Red Cross, the Fellowship of Christian Athletes, the Humane Society, or a political party.

6. Medical

The medical realm is comprised of medicine, phar-maceuticals, research, and science. Medicine is the art and science of healing. It encompasses a range of health care practices evolved to maintain and restore human health by the prevention and treatment of ill-ness. Contemporary medicine applies health science, biomedical research, and medical technology to diag-nose and treat injury and disease, typically through medication, surgery, or some other form of therapy. The word medicine is derived from the Latin *ARS ME-DICINA*, meaning the art of healing. Though medical technology and clinical expertise are pivotal to con-temporary medicine, successful face-to-face relief of actual suffering continues to require the application of ordinary human feeling and compassion, known in English as "bedside manner."

7. Entertainment

Entertainment is also a broad realm that is com-prised of sports, music, dance, clothing, film, travel, modeling, theatre, Hollywood, publishing, exhibition, broadcasting, opera, performing arts, and even the circus. Entertainment is any activity designed to give people pleasure, diversion, or relaxation. An audi-ence may participate in the entertainment passively (as in watching an opera or a movie), or actively (as in playing games). The entertainment industry (much of which is informally known as show business) consists of a large number of sub-industries devoted to entertainment. However, the term is often used in the mass media to describe the mass media conglomerates that control the distribution and manufacture of mass media entertainment. The term "show biz" is associated with the commercially popular performing arts, especially musical theatre, vaudeville, comedy, film, and music.

8. Media

Media is modern communication—radio, TV, newspapers, magazines, journalism, books, advertising, public speaking, broadcasting, editorials, and coverage of the news. The news media refers to the section of the mass media that focuses on presenting current news to the public. These include print media (newspapers, magazines); broadcast media (radio stations, television stations, television networks), and increasingly Internet-based media (websites and the "blogosphere").

9. Internet (E-Commerce)

The Internet represents global communication and now global commerce across the World Wide Web. The Internet is a global system of interconnected computer networks that allow everyday people uncensored access to a vast array of information (and disinformation), goods, and services. The Internet is a "network of networks" that consists of millions of private and public, academic, business, and government networks of local to global scope, all linked together and accessed easily. Imagine life without this quick information resource. Think of the impact of email, on-line chats, file transfers and file sharing (allowing people worlds apart to exchange business logic and data), online gaming, etc. With a web browser (now available in the palm of your hand), a user views web pages that may contain text, images, videos, and other multimedia and navigates between them using hyperlinks. These hyperlinks and URLs allow the web servers and other machines that store originals, and cached copies, of these resources to deliver them as required using HTTP (Hypertext Transfer Protocol). HTTP is only one of the communication protocols used on the Internet (Flash is a newer technology).

10. Real Estate

The realm of real estate includes construction, development, sales, purchases, acquisitions, and property management. Real estate represents wealth, influence, and power. Real estate is a legal term (in some jurisdictions, notably in the USA, United Kingdom, Canada, and Australia) that encompasses land along with anything permanently affixed to the land (such as buildings). Specifically it is property that is stationary or fixed in location.

Real estate law is the body of regulations and legal codes which pertain to such matters under a particular jurisdiction. Real estate is often considered synonymous with real property (also sometimes called realty), in contrast with personal property (also sometimes called chattel or personality under chattel law or personal property law). However, in some situations the term "real estate" refers to the land and fixtures together, as distinguished from "real property," referring to ownership rights of the land itself.

A real estate transaction is the process whereby a property (or designated real estate) is transferred between two or more parties, one being the seller(s) and the other being the buyer(s). It can often be quite complicated due to the size and complexity of the property being transferred, the large amounts of money being exchanged, and complex government regulations. Conventions and requirements also vary considerably among different countries of the world and among the various smaller legal entities with their specific requirements.

11. Culture

Culture is formed through history and trends. Culture is the universal human capacity to classify, codify, and communicate their experiences symbolically. Culture (from the Latin *cultura* stemming from *colere*, meaning *"to cultivate"*) generally refers to patterns of human activity and the symbolic structures that give such activities significance and importance. Cultures can be understood as systems of symbols and meanings that even their creators contest, that lack fixed boundaries, that are constantly in flux, and that interact and compete with one another. Culture can be defined as all the ways of life including arts, beliefs, and institutions of a population that are passed down from generation to generation. Culture has been called "the way of life for an entire society." As such, it includes codes of manners, history, dress, language, religion, rituals, trends, norms of behavior (such as law and morality), and systems of belief as well as the arts. Cultures are internally affected by forces encouraging change as well as by forces resisting change. These forces are related to both social structures and natural events, and are involved in the perpetuation of cultural ideas and practices within current structures, which themselves are subject to change.

12. Invention

Invention is birthed through ideas (witty), new trends, solutions, or patterns. An invention is a new form, composition of matter, device, or process. Some inventions are based on pre-existing forms, compositions, processes, or ideas (an improvement or upgrade, if you will). Other inventions are radical breakthroughs which may extend the boundaries of human knowledge or experience—innovation. Inventions may have a minor impact on society (such as the "Chia Pet") or a major impact on society (such as the Internet), or fall anywhere in between these two extremes. There is also a "cultural invention" which is an innovative set of useful behaviors adopted by people who then pass them on, (such as adopted hygiene practices that affect health and improve the quality and longevity of life). An invention that is novel and not obvious to those who are skilled in the same field may be able to obtain legal protection as intellectual property.

The Number Nine

Nine is the number of finality. It is linked with fullness, with the fruitfulness of the Holy Spirit and the fruit of the womb. The number nine is a most remarkable number in many respects. It is held in great reverence by all who study the occult sciences, and in mathematical science it possesses properties and powers which are found in no other number. Nine is the last of the digits, and thus marks the end. Nine signifies the conclusion of a matter. Nine is akin to the number six—six being the sum of its factors (3 x 3 = 9, and 3 + 3 = 6), and is thus significant of the end of man, and the summation of all man's works. Nine is therefore the number of finality or judgment.

Judgment is committed to Jesus as "the Son of man" (John 5:27; Acts 17:31). It marks completeness, the end and issue of all things pertaining to man—the judgment of man and all his works. Nine is a factor of the number 666 (9 x 74 = 666).

Enough has been said to show that the signification of the number nine is judgment, especially divine judgment, and the conclusion of the whole matter so far as man is concerned.

The Number Three

Nine is the square of three ($3^2 = 9$), and three is the number of Divine perfection, as well as the number peculiar to the Holy Spirit. It is not surprising, therefore, to find that this number denotes finality in divine things. *(Source: The Symbols and Types - Kevin J. Conner)*

In the number three we have quite a new set of phenomena. We come to the first geometrical figure. Two straight lines cannot possibly enclose any space, or form a plane figure, neither can two plane surfaces form a solid. Three lines are necessary to form a plane figure, and the three dimensions of length, breadth, and height, are necessary to form a solid. Hence three is the symbol of the cube—the simplest form of solid figure. As two is the symbol of the square, or plane contents (x^2), so three is the symbol of the cube, or solid contents (x^3).

All things that are specially complete are stamped with this number three. God's attributes are three: omniscience, omnipresence, and omnipotence. There are three great divisions completing time—past, present, and future. There are three persons in grammar and they express and include all the relationships of mankind. Thought, word, and deed, complete the sum of human capability. Three degrees of comparison complete our knowledge of qualities—great, greater, and greatest. The simplest proposition requires three things to complete it—the subject, the predicate, and the direct object.

Three propositions are necessary to complete the simplest form of argument—the major premise, the minor premise, and the conclusion. Three Kingdoms embrace our ideas of matter—animal, vegetable, and mineral. When we turn to the Scriptures, this completion becomes Divine, and marks Divine completeness or perfection.

Three is the first of four perfect numbers (3, 7, 10, and 12):

- *Three* denotes divine perfection;
- *Seven* denotes spiritual perfection;
- *Ten* denotes ordinal perfection; and
- *Twelve* denotes governmental perfection.

Hence the number three points us to what is real, essential, perfect, substantial, complete, and Divine. There is nothing real in man or of man. Everything *"under the sun"* and apart from God is *"vanity." "Every man at his best estate is altogether vanity"* (Psalm 139:5,11, 62:9, 144:4; Ecclessiastes 1:2,4, 2:11,17,26, 3:19, 4:4, 11:8, 12:8; Romans 8:20).

Three is the number associated with the Godhead, for there are "three persons in one God." Three times the Seraphim cry, "Holy, Holy, Holy"—one for each of the three persons in the Trinity (Isaiah 6:3). It is also the number of the living creatures (Revelation 4:8).

Three is the number of resurrection. It was on the third day that Jesus rose from the dead. This was

Divine in operation, and Divine in its prophetic fore-showing in the person of Jonah (Matt 12:39,40; Luke 11:29; Jonah 1:17). It was the third day on which Jesus was "perfected" (Luke 13:32).

The Number Twenty-Seven

Twenty-seven is a multiple of nine (3 x 9 = 27). There are three specific sets of nine that combine to make twenty-seven. I want to cover these three sets of nine: Gifts of the Father, Gifts of the Holy Spirit, and finally, the Gifts of the Son.

The Gifts of the Father

The first nine come from the nine gifts of the Father (the Fruit of the Spirit) found in Galatians 5:22. These gifts have already been given to us and we just need to use them. These 9 gifts are;

Love	*Joy*	*Peace*
Long Suffering	*Gentleness*	*Goodness*
Faith	*Meekness*	*Temperance*

For a complete breakdown and Greek definition of all nine Gifts of the Holy Spirit please visit *www.CrackingTheApostolicAndPropheticCode.com*. Then, visit our web store for even more resources.

The Gifts of the Holy Spirit

The next set of nine gifts that make up our twenty-seven comes from the nine gifts of the Holy Spirit (the Gifts of the Spirit) found in 1 Corinthians 12:8. These gifts have also already been given to us, we just need to receive them. These gifts are;

Word of Wisdom   Word of Knowledge

Discerning of Spirits   Gift of Faith

Gifts of Healing   Working of Miracles

Gift of Prophecy   Diverse Kinds of Tongues

Interpretation of Tongues

These gifts naturally and spiritually break up into three categories.

- ○ Category One: REVELATION—Those gifts that show (or reveal) something. (Word of Wisdom, Word of Knowledge, and Discerning of Spirits).

- ○ Category Two: POWER—Those gifts that do (or activate) something. (Faith, Working of Miracles, and Gifts of Healing).

- ○ Category Three: INSPIRATION—Those gifts that say (or declare) something. (Prophecy, Gift of Tongues, and Gift of Interpretation of Tongues).

Now I will give a very brief description of these important Gifts of the Holy Spirit.

Word of Wisdom

The Word of Wisdom is the revealing of the prophetic future under the anointing of God. It is not your own thinking or ideas.

Word of Knowledge

The Word of Knowledge is the revealing of a fact in existence which cannot be seen, heard, or revealed naturally. It is in existence, it is a fact, it is a knowledge, and it is supernaturally revealed by God. It is the past up until now (thus containing the present).

Discerning of Spirits

The Discerning of Spirits has to do with the comprehension of the human spirit, as supernaturally revealed by the Holy Ghost. It's not discerning of persons, but of spirits.

Faith

The gift of Faith is at work when, without any human effort, God brings to pass a supernatural thing.

Miracles

The gift of the Working of Miracles occurs when, through the human instrument of hands, eyes, mouth, or feet, a person supernaturally does something by the divine energy of the Holy Spirit. An example would be the incident when Samson killed the lion with his bare hands (Judges 14:6).

Gifts of Healings

The Gifts of Healings—the only plural gift, is when God supernaturally heals the sick through any assigned gift of ministry.

Tongues

The gift of Tongues is the ministry of publicly proclaiming a message from God which is not understood by the person giving it.

Interpretation of Tongues

The gift of Interpretation of Tongues is when, without any mental faculties operating, the message that has been given in another language is interpreted supernaturally by the Spirit. It is a word from the Lord and not an interpretation of what one thinks the church should hear or know.

Prophecy

The gift of Prophecy is the anointed speaking forth of words of edification, exhortation, or comfort to the church supernaturally given from God without human thinking. The purpose of prophecy is to build up, and edify the body of Christ, not to tear down.

The Gifts of the Son

I believe that the last nine gifts are a fresh Present Day Revelation that until now (at the writing of this book) have not been released to the body of Christ. Remember that there are revelations and mysteries that have never been released to previous generations until now through the apostles and prophets. I believe that if the Father has gifts and the Holy Spirit has gifts, then the Son has gifts also! In the beginning, God the Father said, *"Let us (God the Father, God the Son, and God the Holy Spirit) make man in our image and in our likeness"* (Genesis 1:28). I have NEVER heard anyone else discuss, mention, preach, teach, or release these last nine gifts. So, right now, by the power of the prophetic, I release and activate these last nine Gifts of the Son (which is also the personality of the Spirit) into the heart, spirit, mind, and mantle of the reader!

Jesus walked in these nine gifts when He was on the earth (see Matthew 10:5), and as I was writing this book I realized that over the past twenty years, I have also walked in all nine of these gifts. This is why I was successful from the moment that I started my business just two months after I was saved with no money, no experience, and no training. But I did not walk in them in the fullness of the revelation of all nine at the same time. But now, since I began working on this book over a year ago, I am beginning to—and the results are awesome! In order to be successful in the marketplace and in the work place you must operate fully in the revelation of these nine gifts in the Kingdom.

<u>These gifts will be given in their fullness once they are activated in our lives by the revelation and impartation from the teaching and preaching from apostles and prophets, and through the ordination and laying on of hands by them releasing others to rule and reign on behalf of the Kingdom of God!</u> They are given to us by the Son so that we can rule and reign just like He did in His place in the gate of the marketplace and work place! These nine gifts are:

Favor	*Influence*	*Fame*
Wealth	*Gathering*	*Negotiation*
Deliverance	*Trust*	*Vision*

Favor

Favor is something done or granted out of good will, rather than from justice or for remuneration. Favor is a supernatural God-like ability that will grant you access into earthly realms for and from a position of heaven.

Influence

Influence is the capacity or power of persons or things to be a compelling force on or produce effects on the actions, behavior, opinions, etc., of others. Influence will allow you to do what you do, and how you do things will grant you open doors of opportunity.

Fame

Fame is widespread reputation and renown. It is associated with favorable character. The gift of Fame has the same grace and attraction that is on Hollywood's actors, movie stars or entertainers, but your fame will cause others to see the Kingdom and its Christ.

Wealth

Wealth is a great quantity or store of money, valuable possessions, property, or other riches. Wealth is created by solving problems which then will create income streams that never stop, quit, or run out.

Gathering

A gathering is an assembly or meeting. The gift of Gathering is a special ability to gather people or others for the purpose of the Kingdom.

Negotiation

A negotiation is a mutual discussion resulting in an arrangement of the terms of a transaction or agreement. The gift of Negotiation is a supernatural grace to get what you want for yourself and others—but without any manipulation, politics, or corruption.

Deliverance

Deliverance is an act or instance of delivering. The gift of Deliverance will allow for breaking the cycle of failure or the world off of someone or something that would normally not go. This is especially evident when supernatural results come after years of counseling, taking medication, or receiving treatment from a medical professional with little (or temporary) results.

Trust

Trust is reliance on the integrity, strength, ability, surety, etc., of a person or thing. Trust is a grace or gift for those to do business or work with you despite their own fears, facts, prejudices, religion, traditions, experiences, cultures, or beliefs.

Vision

Vision is the act or power of sensing with the eyes. The gift of Vision is the grace to open up the future or have insight into the heavens to see beyond the present or current situation no matter how good or bad it really is.

These three important nines come together and give us the number twenty-seven.

$$9 \text{ Gifts of the Father}$$
$$9 \text{ Gifts of the Holy Spirit}$$
$$+ 9 \text{ Gifts of the Son}$$
$$\overline{27}$$

The Number Five

The number five is the number of grace, atonement, the cross, and five-fold ministries. There were five "I wills" of Satan. There were five wounds of Jesus on the cross, five loaves of the bread of life (Mark 6:38; Luke 9:13-16).

Five is the sum of four and one (4 + 1 = 5). We have had hitherto the three persons of the Godhead, and their manifestation in creation. Now we have a further revelation of a people called out from mankind—redeemed and saved to walk with God from earth to heaven. Hence, redemption follows creation. In as much as in the consequence of the fall of man, creation came under the curse and was "made subject to vanity." Therefore, man and creation must be redeemed. Thus we have:

1. Father   2. Son   3. Spirit

4. Creation   5. Redemption

These are the five great mysteries, and five is therefore, the number of GRACE.

Four is the number of the world. It represents man's weakness, helplessness, and vanity. But, when you add one to four (4 + 1 = 5) a significant Divine strength is added to man's weakness and made perfect in that weakness. In essence, omnipotence is combined with the impotence of earth. This Divine favor is uninfluenced and invincible.

The highest governmental office of our country is the President of the United States. He has his five governmental offices (rulers and protectors) to watch over our nation and the people in our nation.

They are the Army, Navy, Marines, Air Force, and Coast Guard. Look at the five governmental offices of heaven and then take a look at how the military government of the United States is set up. I believe that this will give you a clearer picture, because they have patterned themselves after God's military system. *(For a complete breakdown of each military branch visit: http://en.wikipedia. org/wiki/United_States_armed_forces).*

God is the absolute ruler of heaven and earth. His Commander and Chief of the Universe is Jesus Christ. Jesus (like the President of the United States) also has governmental offices (rulers and protectors) to watch over not just His nation (groups of people), but also over His creation and over every generation. This includes both the natural (physical, seen) realm and the spiritual (heavenly, unseen) realm.

This number comes to us from the five governments or offices found in Ephesians 4:11. Each of these offices represents authority given by God to men, and embodies the hand of God on the earth. These offices are; Apostle, Prophet, Evangelist, Pastor, and Teacher.

Apostle

An apostle is a sent one or an ambassador. One who has been sent on a mission or assignment to a specific region or group by God. One who carries, releases, and reveals revelation on behalf of God. I believe that apostles are God's shepherds over five-fold leaders.

Prophet

A prophet is one who announces the will of God before hand—what will occur in the future. A prophet is a divine messenger or one who speaks on behalf of God. It is one who is granted insight on the mysteries and secrets of God and can communicate them to others.

Evangelist

An evangelist is one who declares the good news and has a unique ability to gather and operate in miracles. This is the same anointing needed and used in sales or for networking.

Pastor

A pastor is a shepherd or someone that watches over a flock. Every husband or father is (and should be) a shepherd. God never intended for pastors to be *over* churches, but to pastor people. Apostles and prophets are to be over churches.

Teacher

Teachers are those who break down truths, teach or instruct, and make disciples.

All of these five-fold gifts work together for the equipping of the saints to do the work of the Kingdom. All are necessary and all important. All must function in order for there to be completeness in God's order.

Add them all up!

We have been discussing the significance of certain numbers and how they are represented throughout the Bible. In chapter one, we discussed the three gates to the Kingdom of Heaven: The *Eclessia* (the *four-walled* Church), The Marketplace, and The Work Place. It is through these gates that we are granted access to the twelve Kingdoms (realms or worlds) discussed earlier. It is by the twenty-seven gifts that we can perform our function and rule and reign in these realms. We rule and reign as kings, operating in God's governmental structure of the five-fold ministry. Now, let's take all of those things together, and add them up.

3 Gates

12 Kingdoms

27 Gifts

+ 5 Offices

47

Let's break down the number forty-seven. If you write it in its expanded form, it is forty plus seven.

$$40 + 7 = 47$$

The Number Forty

The number forty represents generations. Forty is the number of probation and the number of testing (ending in victory or defeat). It rained for forty days and forty nights upon the earth (Genesis 7:12). The Israelites wandered for forty years in the desert (Exodus 16:5; Deuteronomy 2:7). Jesus spent forty days in the wilderness (Mark 1:13). There are many, many references to the number forty in the Bible.

Forty has long been universally recognized as an important number, both on account of the frequency of its occurrence, and the uniformity of its association with a period of probation, trial, and chastisement— (not judgment, like the number nine, which stands in connection with the punishment of enemies, but the chastisement of sons, and of a covenant people). It is the product of five and eight (5 x 8 = 40), and points to the action of grace (number 5), leading to and ending in revival and renewal (number 8). This is certainly the case where forty relates to a period of evident probation. But where it relates to enlarged dominion, or to renewed or extended rule, then it does so in virtue of its factors four and ten, (4 x 10 = 40) and in harmony with their signification. The world and man (number 4) and ordinal perfection (number 10).

40 Years

There are 15 periods of forty years which appear in the Bible, and which may be classified as follows:

- *Forty Years of Probation by Trial:*
  Israel in the wilderness (Deuteronomy 8:2-5; Psalms 95:10; Acts 13:18—the third 40 of Moses' life, 120 years).
  Israel from the crucifixion to the destruction of Jerusalem.

- *Forty Years of Probation by Prosperity in Deliverance and Rest:*
  under Othniel, Judges 3:11,
  under Barak, Judges 5:31,
  under Gideon, Judges 8:28.

- *Forty Years of Probation by Prosperity in Enlarged Dominion:*
  under David, 2 Samuel 5:4,
  under Solomon, 1 Kings 11:42,
  under Jeroboam II. See 2 Kings 12:17,18, 13:3,5,7,22,25, 14:12-14,23,28,
  under Jehoash, 2 Kings 12:1,
  under Joash, 2 Chronicles 24:1.

- *Forty Years of Probation by Humiliation and Servitude:*
  Israel under the Philistines, Judges 13:1.
  Israel in the time of Eli, 1 Samuel 4:18.
  Israel under Saul, Acts 13:21.

○ *Forty Years of Probation by Waiting:*
Moses in Egypt, Acts 7:23.
Moses in Midian, Acts 7:30

40 Days

There are eight periods of forty days described in the Bible:

○ Forty days Moses was in the mount (Exodus 24:18); and to receive the Law (Exodus 24:18).

○ Forty days Moses was in the mount after the sin of the Golden Calf (Deuteronomy 9:18,25).

○ Forty days of the spies, issuing in the penal sentence of the 40 years (Numbers 13:26, 14:34).

○ Forty days of Elijah in Horeb (1 Kings 19:8).

○ Forty days of Jonah and Nineveh (Jonah 3:4).

○ Forty days Ezekiel lay on his right side to symbolize the 40 years of Judah's transgression. Note: 40 becomes a number closely connected with Judah, as 390 (Ezekiel 4:5) is the number of separated Israel.

○ Forty days Jesus was tempted of the Devil (Matthew 4:2).

○ Forty days Jesus was seen of His disciples, speaking of the things pertaining to the Kingdom of God (Acts 1:2).

The children of Israel wandered for forty years, but because of their division, disobedience, murmuring, complaining, confusion, disrespect of covenant, and poverty mindset, God allowed an ENTIRE GENERATION to die in the wilderness (a place of insignificance). Only a remnant or two people from that generation (Joshua and Caleb) were allowed to enter the Promised Land. God allowed them to live for these reasons: 1. Because they obeyed the prophet; 2. Because someone in every generation no matter the circumstances or the economy is always entitled to live in the promises of God and possess their inheritance; 3. So that the next generation could receive their inheritance.

Any man, woman, ministry, business, or group of people that is not focused on the next generation will not stand the test of time. If you can fulfill or complete your vision, dream, business, ministry, or idea in YOUR LIFETIME, I guarantee that it did not come from God. In Psalm 145:9-13 He said, *"The LORD is good to all: and His tender mercies are over all his works. All thy works shall praise thee, O LORD; and Thy saints shall bless Thee. They shall speak of the glory of Thy kingdom, and talk of Thy power; To make known to the sons of men His mighty acts, and the glorious majesty of His kingdom. Thy kingdom is an everlasting kingdom, and thy dominion ENDURETH THROUGHOUT ALL GENERATIONS!"*

Take a look at Ephesians 3:20-21, *"Now unto Him that is able to do exceeding abundantly above all that we ask or think, according to the power that worketh in us, Unto Him be glory in the church by Christ Jesus throughout all ages, and world without end. AMEN!"*

When I finished reading this verse and I looked at the word amen with an exclamation mark, I get a mental picture of when a football player makes it into the end zone and spikes or slams the ball on the ground. That player is stating, "I made it past all of your players and they gave me their best defense, but it still wasn't enough to stop me from getting in the end zone (my Promised Land)!"

It is not enough for us to just be successful, we must pass the torch on to our children, grandchildren, and to our spiritual sons and daughters while we are still alive on the earth. This is so that future generations will not fail, fall, or compromise until the kingdoms of this world have become the Kingdom of our God. Future generations of saints will rule and reign in the earth with greater power, greater authority, and greater revelation because we launched them from our shoulders, passing on our wisdom, knowledge, and experience.

The Number Seven

Now, let's look at the number seven. Seven is the number of spiritual perfection, the number of completion, and revelation. God created the earth in six days and He rested on the seventh day or in the revelation of what He created (Genesis 2:2). Webster's defines the word rested as: to refrain from labor or exertion; to be free from anxiety or disturbance; to remain confident; to remain for action or accomplishment; to cause to be firmly fixed; having peace of mind or spirit.

If you search the number seven in the Bible, it was used about 600 times. It is an important number.

Now, let's take forty plus seven and add to that, another three. (This three is representative of the three gates of hell discussed in chapter two; religion, tradition and racism). The result is fifty.

$$40 + 7 + 3 = 50$$

The Number Fifty

The number fifty is the number of Pentecost, liberty, freedom, and jubilee. Fifty represents fresh fire and new language (Acts 2:1), and is the number of Pentecost. It is a new entry into the marketplace and all of the known worlds. Every fifty years was the Year of Jubilee (Leviticus 25). The Year of Jubilee allows for emancipation of slaves, forgiveness of debts, and return of property. Fifty is a number of deliverance. Fifty represents a time of harvest and celebration. It is a release for global dominance of all the world's systems. It's a national and cultural call for ALL to come and celebrate.

Falling into Place

As I mentioned, the more I studied these numbers and the more I sought for revelation regarding dominion, destiny, and authority, the more these numbers took on significance. I looked at the numbers I studied; 12, 27, 5, 3, 47, 40, 7, 3 (again), and 50. When I got to the number fifty, I noticed that I had nine groups of numbers.

I don't want to get lost in numerology, or come across as being strange or "cooky." However, I do want you to think about all of these things prophetically. They have prophetic significance. There are nine groups of numbers here and nine is a number that represents finality, fullness, and fruitfulness. The nine groups of numbers end at fifty which represents liberty and freedom. When the Holy Ghost fell on the Day of Pentecost, the first liberty that apostles and the 120 that were gathered together in the upper room received was the ability to speak every man's language in the marketplace (Acts 2:1-8).

Line up all these things into place and look at them with prophetic insight. There are twelve Kingdoms; Education, Government, Technology, Financial, Society, Medicine, Entertainment, Media, Internet, Real Estate, Culture, and Invention. These are accessed through one of the three gates of heaven; *Eclessia*, Marketplace or Work Place. Access to take dominion in these Kingdoms can be hindered or lost through the strongholds (or gates) of hell; Religion, Tradition, or Racism.

Now, stay with me. There are five heavenly governmental offices set up on earth by Jesus Christ Himself; Apostle, Prophet, Evangelist, Pastor and Teacher. All of these offices are just now fully restored on the earth. The stage is set and it is time for us to move into completion and fullness out of the *four-walled* church as apostles and prophets and no longer just as Christian business owners or Christians doing business.

There has been testing and training for many years, and God has a remnant that has been released out of the *four-walled* church so that now many sons and daughters (as the next generation) can finally be released into the apostolic and the prophetic. It is now time to enter into our year and season of Jubilee. It is time for us to move out into the territory, industry, calling, and five-fold office that Jesus Christ has already established—our Promised Land. Our land is the marketplace via the Kingdom of Heaven where we are authorized and commissioned (sent apostolically) to rule and reign as His Kingdom representatives as apostles and prophets with Kingdom authority!

There is no longer any need to tarry like the early church had to in order to receive the Holy Ghost, because this is not only that which was prophesied and released on the Day of Pentecost, but also what Jesus already released when He ascended on high and gave gifts to man (Ephesians 4:8-11). They ARE the SAME five gifts (mantles, graces, and offices) that He walked in, lived in, and operated in during his earthly ministry and NOW THESE GIFTS HAVE BEEN GIVEN TO YOU!

Consider this, when Jesus left planet earth He did not take these gifts (mantles, graces, offices) back with Him—He released them! Now we know why so many other great men and women of God that had powerful ministries with signs and wonders, whose ministries (upon their death) failed or stopped. They did not release their mantles (gifts) upon their spiritual sons and daughters while they were alive in order that future generations could rule the world with them (exercising their gifts)! I remember in 1997, I was an armor bearer for Prophet Mark Chironna for several days. The last day, when I dropped him back off at his hotel, I asked him this question? "What happened to the mantels of those who had previously walked in the prophetic, signs and wonders, had great anointings to create great sums of wealth and have died?" I went on to say, "It seems as if those mantles are just lying around, left here on the earth and if so, is it possible to just pick them up?" He smiled and said, "Absolutely."

When those men or women died and their mantles were not passed on, they fell back to the earth. It is up to every generation (even if it is just a remnant) to begin to pick them up and use them so that we can begin to rule and reign! I charge you today not only to begin to pick up the mantle of apostles, prophets, and kings which have been lost for generations, but we must also pass them on to the next generation while we are still alive.

ℬ ℭ

CONCLUSION

ℬ ℭ

Once you take a moment to let this all sink in, and your spirit bears witness that this paradigm is indeed scriptural, you can confidently embrace this revelation. You are now poised to take your place in advancing the Kingdom of God on the earth—then you can pass it on to the next generation!

The *Eclessia*

Order in the church must come. There needs to be recognition that dominion and release is God's order. The church must function to edify and equip, raise up and release people to move into their realms and rule and reign with the authority of God. Let me ask you a question. Why do you think God Himself (along with God the Son, and God the Holy Spirit) personally gave mankind DOMINION to rule on the earth BEFORE the *four-walled* church, its systems or pastors were EVER created or established? God knew that man would mess up, but the moment you UNDERSTAND who you are, Whose you are, and what your assignment is, and then you are set (back) in your place by an apostle or prophet, the earth belongs to you. It has always been yours from the day the earth was created for you to personally and individually rule and reign. You first do this through your family. That is why He said, *"be fruit-ful, and multiply, and replenish the earth, and subdue it: and have dominion over it..."* (Genesis 1:28). Remember, the first thing that Jesus said when He came out of the wilderness was to repent (turn around) for the KINGDOM OF HEAVEN IS AT HAND! Every person that followed Him received their inheritance—a piece of the earthly realm and the heavenly realm. God's intent is that every saint or believer would rule and reign on the earth! If you are a *four-walled* church leader or a pastor, God never intended for you to rule over people, but to rule among them so that they could receive their inheritance on your watch.

The MarketPlace

As a Christian business owner, you must embrace your role as an apostle or prophet. You can not continue business as usual. If your *four-walled* church leader or pastor does not have a Kingdom mentality or vision, or if they do not believe in the five-fold office or ministry gifts, if they will not release you or others outside of the four walls, then you may need to consider your connection with their covering. You will have to embrace the ministry of apostles and prophets yourself! If you are a Kingdom Representative in a territory, an apostolic assignment is implied. It is no longer enough to just be a Christian in business or a Christian doing business. To be successful in the marketplace requires unlocking the apostolic and prophetic code and running your business in a way you have never done before. Remember, the Kingdom of Heaven and the Kingdom of God are made up of the earthly realm and the heavenly realm and YOU ARE THE GOVERNMENTAL RULER!

The Work Place

The twelve Kingdoms are touched everyday by the work place. Those called to the work place must stop seeing the church as their only territory for ministry. You have been called to exercise dominion in the territory and occupation where you function and work. If you work as a nurse, then you are called to impact the realm of medicine. If you are a teacher, then influence the realm of education. As a CEO, you are touching and influencing the economy. Whatever you do, whatever your assignment and giftings, you are touching one or more of the twelve Kingdoms and you have been sent (apostolically and prophetically) to exercise dominion in that sphere of influence.

"And He called his ten servants, and delivered them ten pounds, and said unto them, Occupy till I come."

Luke 19:13

The word occupy means to "do business" until I come!

"Wherefore the rather, brethren, give diligence to make your calling and election sure: for if ye do these things, ye shall never fall."

2 Peter 1:10

Why the Code Matters

Understanding the apostolic and prophetic code gives you clarity of your purpose and authorization to fulfill it. You must open yourself up to a new way of thinking and a new way of being in covenant and ministry related relationships. They must be direct. They can NO LONGER just be through your local church or pastor. You must allow yourself not only to become apostolic and prophetic, but you must financially sow into the ministry of apostles and prophets that God links you to and connects you with—even if you have a pastor or if you tithe to a local church. Your life and future will depend on it. When you study the life of the apostles and prophets in both the Old and New Testament, those that committed and sowed their finances (or resources) into their lives directly received "upgrades" that couldn't have come any other way or from any other source.

Today you and I must not only be open to sow our finances, but also open to tithe (whether it is a partial tithe or a whole tithe) into apostles and prophets for impartation, covering, revelation, and for their govern-mental grace and authority that God has mandated for your life, family, business, city, and ministry. If you are bound by religion or tradition, or if you are trapped in a controlling hierarchy of ministerial relationships, this will seem CRAZY. I present to you that if you can't do what you believe God wants you to do, and do it with the person whom He wants you to do it with, THAT is CRAZY! It's a new day. It's a new time for us to rise up and establish covenant relationships so that we can change the world that we live in. You can't reap were you have not sowed!

If we are to take our dominion in the earth and in-fluence every area, a reformation of thought patterns is required. Throughout the Bible, God asks people to do things that He never asked anyone else to do be-fore. Why do we think it is any different today? God can speak to you as He has never spoken to anyone else before. In fact, this is exactly what He wants to do! His assignment for you is not a carbon copy of His assignment for someone else. It is as unique and spe-cial as your thumbprint. <u>This is why you must embrace the apostolic and the prophetic, because it is the only thing that can take you to a place that you have never been before!</u>

Lastly, I want to leave you with five Scriptures that will bless you, shift you, and empower you.

Jesus said, "Ye are my friends, if ye do whatsoever I command you. Henceforth I call you not servants; for the servant knoweth not what his lord doeth: but I have called you friends; for all things that I have heard of my Father I have made known unto you. Ye have not chosen me, but I have chosen you, and ordained you, that ye should go and bring forth fruit, and that your fruit should remain: that whatsoever ye shall ask of the Father in My name, He may give it you.

John 15:14-16

And in that day ye shall ask Me nothing. Verily, verily, I say unto you, Whatsoever ye shall ask the Father in My name, He will give it you. Hitherto have ye asked nothing in My name: ask, and ye shall receive, that your joy may be full. These things have I spoken unto you in proverbs: but the time cometh, when I shall no more speak unto you in proverbs, but I shall shew you plainly of the Father. At that day ye shall ask in My name: and I say not unto you, that I will pray the Father for you: For the Father Himself loveth you, because ye have loved Me, and have believed that I came out from God. I came forth from the Father, and am come into the world: again, I leave the world, and go to the Father.

John 16:23-28

And this is the confidence that we have in Him, that, if we ask ANY THING according to His will, He heareth us: And if we know that He hear us, whatsoever we ask, we know that we have the petitions (decrees or request of the Kingdom) that we desired of Him.

1 John 5:14-15

Thus saith the LORD, the Holy One of Israel, and His Maker, Ask Me of things to come concerning My sons, and concerning the work of My hands command ye Me.

Isaiah 45:11

Call unto me, and I will answer thee,
and shew thee great and mighty
things, which thou knowest not.

Jeremiah 33:3

The Amplified Bible says, "fenced in and hidden things that you do not know about." In other words, when you call Me (God), I will show you what part of the world that I have put up a fence around—this is the land in your name that I created for you to rule and reign on!

Hebrews 11 says that many people received great things and had great accomplishments "through faith." *"Through faith"* they even subdued kingdoms, obtained promises, stopped the mouths of lions, escaped the edge of the sword, the dead were raised to life again, and others were tortured, not accepting deliverance that they might obtain a better resurrection. It goes on to say that, ***"these all died in faith, not having received the promises, but having seen them afar off..."***

All you have to do is see it and seize it! I want to encourage you that by faith you now have the right to operate in the Kingdom using the apostolic and pro-phetic code so that you can claim, walk in, and receive ALL of the promises of God today!

What is faith? It is the substance (tangible evidence) of things hoped for that were seen afar off in previous generations that are FINIALLY HERE NOW—RIGHT NOW,

IN OUR DAY! Faith is knowledge or a know-how in God. We have faith, because we know God. Your faith is not based on you. It is not measured by just your experiences, but on God's experiences in the earth and in the heavenly realm. Whatever He has done for someone else (in this or in previous generations) He wants to do even MORE for you TODAY! It is His nature. So my desire and my goal for you was to release and impart a present day truth and revelation that would allow your faith to PRODUCE a "Tangible Evidence" over all of the world systems!

To the next generation (the world calls you "GenerationX," but I call you the "NOW Generation") and to your children: It took me more than twenty years to walk out this revelation and fully understand it. With the technology readily available to you, with your energy and your passion, I place the revelation of the Kingdom in this book into your hands—now, **go rule and reign with it!**

I hope that you enjoyed reading this book just as much as I have enjoyed writing it and living in its revelation for more than twenty years. I encourage you to be devoted to your spouse, dedicated to your children, and committed to your calling.

Establishing and Releasing Kings To Take Over!
Prophet Craig A. Ponder, Sr., CEA
Prophet Darlene Ponder

꙰ ꙮ

ABOUT THE AUTHOR

꙰ ꙮ

Before his salvation experience, Craig Ponder was facing thirteen years in prison, was sentenced to five and a half years, and ended up serving two years. During one season, he stayed awake for eighteen days straight and on December 6, 1987, weighing only 122 pounds, the Lord revealed to him that he only had fourteen days left to live. That day he made a decision to give his life to the Lord. Two weeks later, on his twenty-fourth birthday, he married his wife, Darlene, who he has been with since age nineteen. It was because of her prayers, decrees, and spiritual influence that Craig was won over to Christ.

Two months after Craig was saved, the Lord called him into the Marketplace and told him to start a business. So, he went to his pastor, received counsel, and started a gardening and lawn service company—with no money or equipment. He simply stepped out by faith on a prophetic promise from God. Craig grew that company from nothing to employing more than nine people, a fleet of six trucks, and the business grossed over one million dollars in sales in six years.

Three months after he was saved, the Lord called him into the five-fold ministry to be a prophet to the nations (Isaiah 61) and he has flowed effectively in the prophetic with accuracy, clarity, and under an open heaven. His prophetic mantle and gift has helped those he has come in contact with—to shift them from where they are personally, financially, spiritually, and mentally to where God has already established them to be. They didn't know how to get there until after the prophetic release from the prophet's mantle.

Prophet Craig was one of the first blacks and one of the youngest ministers to receive credentials from the denomination he was connected with when he was first saved. He served there as a leader and associate pastor for eight years. (Prophet Craig has been licensed as a minister since 1988, and was first ordained as a pastor in 1999 and again in 2002 by Apostle John Eckhardt and another apostle.

Prophet Craig has a heart for God's people, and loves to advance the Kingdom of God in the Marketplace. He also has had the privilege throughout the years to serve as an armor bearer for some of the greatest apostles, prophets, and pastors that God is using throughout the earth.

As bold and authoritative as he is in the spirit realm and in the natural realm, he is just as equally humble. He is the type of person that you will either love or hate—and even those that hate him respect him, because he leaves them in a better position than they were in when they met him. With his confrontational and direct approach, you never have to guess what he is thinking or where he is going—you will always know.

Shortly after he was saved, the Lord took him in the spirit and showed him his future. At the end of the open vision, he was standing in front of an office building that was over ten stories high. Craig asked the Lord, "What is that?" The Lord said, "This is what you will need if you abide in my word." Prophet Craig is still waiting for that building to manifest.

In 1992, Prophet Craig sold his gardening and lawn service company and started a marketing, insurance, and financial services firm to reach the market of the self-employed and middle Americans. Today he is the CEO and Founder of *WealthBuildersAdvisoryGroup.com*, a national financial services firm that shows Americans, Baby Boomers, Christians, Home Owners and the Self-Employed how to grow their wealth every year! They do this "No Matter What Is Going On In The STOCK and REAL ESTATE Markets." Not only do they grow wealthier, but they help their clients reduce their taxes and protect their equity—guaranteed!

Prophet Craig has helped countless numbers of people start their own business, get it to the next level, and achieve their financial goals. He and his wife, Prophet Darlene, have successfully started and owned more than twelve businesses over the past twenty years.

They have an anointing to impart present day truth, encouragement, confirmation, and a liberty to help release the body of Christ fulfill their destiny, build a successful marriage, create wealth, become financially free. They also help them connect to the local church, learning how to be used effectively in the Marketplace and the five-fold office that God had called them to.

This dynamic couple is anointed and they carry a message and a burden to shift the church and establish the Kingdom of God by helping pastors, congregations, and other five-fold leaders shift their leaders. They release them to *"MantleShift"*—that is, to move into their apostolic and prophetic call and role for their territory, region, industry, and into the realm of wealth which will cause social, economic, and spiritual dominion for their church members and in their city.

Craig and Darlene Ponder have been together for almost twenty-six years, having been married for more than twenty of those years. They have three handsome sons; Robert, Craig Jr., and Matthew, all serving

God. Their daughter-in-law, Christina, is an emerging prophetess and has blessed them with two grandsons, Nathaniel and David. Craig loves to jog every day at the ocean with his boxer dog, Bruce Lee. He enjoys taking numerous vacations and likes to relax with his family on their boat that is slipped in the Oceanside, California Harbor.

In 2001, Craig was involved in two major rollover accidents where he almost died. He and Darlene were pastoring full time in San Bernardino, CA during this time. In 2002, the Lord instructed them to close their church down and relocate to Oceanside, CA. There they began working with an apostle and his church and served the next several years in leadership as deacon, care pastors, an ordained minister as well as a marketplace minister.

Prophet Craig A. Ponder Sr., CEA, has been successful in business for over twenty-four years. He has been a Wealth Strategist and an Info-Preneur for fifteen years. He is a Certified Estate Advisor through the National Association of Financial and Estate Advisors (NAFEP), a member of Freedom Equity Group (a national secular group of wealth builders), a member of the Asset Protection Society, and he is also a HERO Solutions Advisor™ with Marion Snow, the New York Times #1 National Best Selling Author of, "*Stop Sitting On Your Assets.*" Craig's firm is also associated with Freedom Tax Advisors, Inc., a national group of advisors with over 240 offices nationwide that specialize in taxes, retirement, and investment strategies for seniors and Baby Boomers. Prophet Craig is also a member of Apostle John P. Kelly's, International Christian Wealth-Builders Foundation. John Kelly serves as a vital part of their apostolic vision.

Prophet Craig is considered by some to be a "Minister of Finances" and a "Prophet of Wealth" that God is using and has raised up in these "Present Days" to help manage, facilitate, create, and transfer the wealth from the world, through the church, and into the Kingdom of God for the benefit of social, economic, and Kingdom dominion.

Prophet Craig was ordained as a Prophet on June 30, 2007 by Apostle John Eckhardt, and is a member of IMPACT Network with Apostle John Eckhardt being his primary spiritual covering. Prophets Craig and Darlene are a part of the Prophetic and Apostolic Company with Apostle John Eckhardt and the IMPACT Network. They hold weekly Prophetic Gatherings and seminars which bring upgrades, advancement, and deliverance.

After being involved with established ministry in the local church for nineteen years, Prophets Craig and Darlene were released by God (November 2006) to walk in their office as a prophet and apostle to help others walk in their dominion covenant in their five-fold calling in the marketplace, the work place, the *four-walled* church, their territory, industry or their sphere of influence.

On June 28, 2008, Craig & Darlene received their apostolic commission to pioneer their new church, located in Carlsbad, CA, KingdomGenerationInternational.com. Now they both walk in their offices as apostles and prophets as they are raising up a church for the next generation.

Prophets Craig and Darlene's apostolic, prophetic, and kingly mantle will shift you into your apostolic and prophetic call. This will cause spiritual, social, covenantal, and financial dominion to begin to take place in your life immediately! Their mission is: **"To Establish and Release Kings To Take Over!"**

If you would like to learn more about Craig and Darlene Ponder, their ministry, or their business, please visit and bookmark the following websites below:

www.CrackingTheApostolicAndPropheticCode.com

www.PropheticGathering.com

www.FinancialWarning.com

www.MoveMyMoneyNow.com

If you would like to schedule Apostle Craig A. Ponder, Sr., CEA or Prophet Darlene Ponder for a Conference, Seminar, or Speaking Engagement, please contact them at:

Kingdom Generation International.com
2111 El Camino Real Suite 202
Oceanside, CA 92054
800-908-7095
Fax: 800-315-0238
email: Info@KingdomGenerationInternational.com

My family and I are looking forward to getting to know you as we establish God's Kingdom together and watch you and your family fulfill the call of God for your life and create the wealth that has been set aside in the earthly realm for you!

If you or someone you know ever needed a reason to move or relocate to southern California, we are making a national call for Singers, Musicians, Psalmists, Minstrels, Families, Youth, Entrepreneurs, Business Owners, Women, Leaders, and those that feel called to the Five-Fold Ministry to help take our territory (San Diego County) and the surrounding regions (Orange and Riverside Counties) for the Kingdom of God!

Apostle Craig and Prophet Darlene Ponder

This COMPILED INFORMATION has never before been made available to the general public until NOW! It is GUARANTEED to save you tens of thousands of dollars in taxes and increase your retirement nest-egg by hundreds of thousands of dollars—GUARANTEED!

Client Testimony

Craig I'd like to personally thank you and your Advisory Group for what you did for me. You took my existing mortgage and reduced it by $2300.00 a month when the mortgage broker that I had worked with for over 10 years could only reduce it by $500.00 a month. You then restructured all of my investments so that I wouldn't out live my income and you guaranteed my principal against market loss! Being a single female I can't tell you how much it means to find someone like you that really care about the people that you work with I just wish I would have found you 15 years ago.

—Mary H, Costa Mesa, CA

Find Out How To Get A FREE $5200.00 Financial Review!

To get the full details right now or to find out more regarding the $100,000 Guarantee and the $2000 Challenge, please visit:

www.BabyBoomerRetirementSolutions.com

www.CraigPonder.com